Serving More Than Students:
A Critical Need for College Student Personnel Services

by Peter H. Garland

ASHE-ERIC Higher Education Report No. 7, 1985

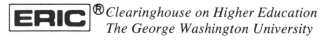

Prepared by

 *®Clearinghouse on Higher Education*
The George Washington University

Published by

Association for the Study of Higher Education

Jonathan D. Fife,
Series Editor

Cite as
Garland, Peter H. *Serving More Than Students: A Critical Need for College Student Personnel Services*. ASHE-ERIC Higher Education Report No. 7. Washington, D.C.: Association for the Study of Higher Education, 1985.

The ERIC Clearinghouse on Higher Education invites individuals to submit proposals for writing monographs for the Higher Education Report series. Proposals must include:
1. A detailed manuscript proposal of not more than five pages.
2. A 75-word summary to be used by several review committees for the initial screening and rating of each proposal.
3. A vita.
4. A writing sample.

Library of Congress Catalog Card Number 86-070252
ISSN 0884-0040
ISBN 0-913317-26-8

ERIC® **Clearinghouse on Higher Education**
The George Washington University
One Dupont Circle, Suite 630
Washington, D.C. 20036

ASHE **Association for the Study of Higher Education**
One Dupont Circle, Suite 630
Washington, D.C. 20036

This publication was partially prepared with funding from the National Institute of Education, U.S. Department of Education under contract no. 400-82-0011. The opinions expressed in this report do not necessarily reflect the positions or policies of NIE or the Department.

EXECUTIVE SUMMARY

Colleges and universities today are confronted with a variety of changing conditions that demand attention; indeed, the formulation of appropriate and effective responses to a changing world has become increasingly important to the survival and viability of institutions. Changes in society, in the higher education enterprise, and in the types and characteristics of students are among those issues that must be addressed.

Increasingly, the efforts of student affairs aimed at improving quality of life, integrating new student groups, and attracting and retaining students are becoming critical to institutions attempting to maintain enrollments of qualified students, assure placement of graduates, develop supportive alumni, and enhance academic involvement. Institutions' employment of these strategies in response to changing conditions creates opportunities for student affairs professionals to become leaders within the institution as they offer important contributions to institutional vitality. This time is a significant period in the evolution of student affairs.

To What Changes Must Student Affairs Organizations Respond?

Institutions and their student affairs organizations are confronted with various changes in their contexts and clienteles. The first group of these trends, leading to change in society, is witnessed by a decreasing birth rate, growth of minority subpopulations, the evolving information society, growing narcissism, and the legacy of the baby boom. Second, institutions and student affairs must respond to changes in the higher education enterprise—changing financial conditions, increased planning, increased judicial intervention, and the growing application of management techniques to higher education. Third, students are changing. Minority participation is growing, vocationalism is increasing, and students' characteristics, values, and needs are changing.

In What Ways Can Student Affairs Take Leadership in Strategies to Respond to Changing Conditions?

In response to changing conditions, institutions are devoting efforts to managing enrollments, using institutional marketing strategies to attract new student clienteles and to retain current students; increasing private funding; planning carefully and managing resources effectively; modifying programs and services to meet changing needs; and introducing activities aimed at enhancing students' involvement in college life.

Current efforts support the increasing congruity between the goals of student affairs and the goals of the institution; efforts by student affairs organizations aimed at the individual and group development, student integration, and student involvement, once regarded as peripheral to the academic mission of the institution (McConnell 1970), have become increasingly important to institutions in their efforts to enhance institutional vitality. Student affairs departments are enhancing the involvement of students in the academic experience, engaging in preventive law, integrating new student groups, participating in the recruitment and retention of students, and helping to develop supportive alumni (Baldridge, Kemerer, and Green 1982). As student affairs professionals achieve institutional support in their pursuit of the traditional goals of student development, recognition of an expanded role for student affairs is demanded.

What New Role Is Emerging for Student Affairs?
The student affairs organization shares the orientations of the three major campus groups—faculty, students, and administrators—and its position on the borders of these groups may be its greatest strength (Silverman 1980).

Our uniqueness as student personnel workers rests on our ability to fashion significant educational environments, using the resources, values, norms, and opportunities of the variety of constituencies on our campuses. To the extent that we are successful in our innovative work, we will be respected, not because of position, but as a result of the impacts we have on campus life. Truly, student personnel workers have the opportunities to be central figures for campus improvement in an era when resources must be perceived as newly combined rather than as new (Silverman 1980, p. 12).

The term ''integrator'' is appropriate for the student affairs professional who integrates student development and institutional development.

"An alert, assertive response to these forces [changing conditions] will make student affairs essential to institutional effectiveness and therefore worthy of adequate support" (Shaffer 1984, p. 112). Recognition of the importance of student affairs to institutional vitality is growing, and student affairs administrators must assume leadership in formulating and managing institutional responses to changing conditions.

Serving as integrators of goals within institutions, student affairs professionals will become more centrally involved in the direction of the institution if they are able to build stronger bridges to the academic and administrative communities. The challenges are many, but student affairs professionals have the opportunity to lead efforts that will affect the entire institution. And goals, priorities, and values will be better integrated as a result of those efforts.

What Implications Does This New Role Have for Student Affairs?

A new role for student affairs calls for changes in the programs and services offered by student affairs, the professional skills required by student affairs administrators, and the content of the preparation and development of professionals. Several programs and services stand to be enhanced by the changing role: enrollment management, programs and services designed to serve the needs of nontraditional students, and activities designed to enhance career planning and placement.

To assume a stronger position of leadership within the institution, student affairs professionals must possess a wider repertoire of skills. In addition to the traditional skills in human relations, student affairs professionals must develop the organizational skills demanded by an expanded role within the institution, including those directed at general management and planning, resource management, information management, institutional politics, and research and evaluation.

The development of new skills for student affairs professionals has clear implications for the preparation and continuing professional education of individuals in the profession. Currently, most preparation programs and recommended curricula for the preparation of new professionals concentrate on counseling and the human relations skills necessary for entry-level practitioners and pay little attention to the administrative or organizational skills demanded by the emerging role of integrator. A changing role for student affairs demands different skills. Therefore, graduate programs at both the master's and doctoral levels must embrace such topics as organizational behavior and development, management and planning in higher education, and the development of higher education. Further, continuing professional education must work toward the development and enhancement of these skills in an organized and comprehensive fashion.

A new role also creates challenges for the application of student development. If student development is to offer guidance to the profession and become more useful to the student affairs integrator, then several issues must be addressed: (1) the understanding and application of student development within the field to enhance the theoretical credibility of student affairs professionals; (2) the expansion of student development theory to encompass increasing numbers of nontraditional students; and (3) the integration of student and organizational development (Borland 1980).

To better serve as integrators within the institution, student affairs professionals must:

1. assess the environment of the institution
2. comprehend institutional issues and internal politics
3. develop professional credibility with faculty
4. become experts on students' expectations, needs, and interests and be able to articulate them to others in the institution
5. be able to explain the goals of student affairs and student development to others in the institution in terms that are meaningful to them
6. contribute to the quality of the academic experience
7. contribute to the effective and efficient management of the institution and be prepared to take leadership in the formulation of institutional responses to changing conditions
8. develop appropriate skills.

Furthermore, institutions, if they are to take advantage of the real and potential contributions of student affairs staff should:

1. recognize, enhance, and support the efforts of student affairs
2. consider student affairs full partners in the institution
3. challenge student affairs professionals to make greater contributions to the institution.

In addition, student personnel preparation programs must be revised to develop the skills necessary for the profession, including greater attention to management and organizational skills. And finally, the national associations for student affairs must:

1. provide direction for new professional roles
2. promote continuing professional education at all levels.

ADVISORY BOARD

CONSULTING EDITORS

Richard Alfred
Associate Professor and Chair
Graduate Program in Higher and Adult Continuing Education
University of Michigan

Robert H. Atwell
President
American Council on Education

Robert Barak
Deputy Executive Secretary
Director of Academic Affairs and Research
Iowa State Board of Regents

Larry A. Braskamp
Assistant to the Vice Chancellor for Academic Affairs
University of Illinois

Robert Cope
Professor of Higher Education
University of Washington

John W. Creswell
Associate Professor
Department of Educational Administration
University of Nebraska

Mary Frank Fox
Assistant Research Scientist
Center for Research on Social Organization
University of Michigan

Timothy Gallineau
Vice President for Student Development
Saint Bonaventure University

W. Lee Hansen
Professor
Department of Economics
University of Wisconsin

David Kaser
Professor
School of Library and Information Science
Indiana University

CONTENTS

Foreword	**xv**
Acknowledgments	**xvii**
The Evolving Role of Student Affairs	**1**
The Disciplinarian	3
The Custodian	4
The Educator	5
The Role of Student Affairs Today	7
A Changing Society	**11**
A Declining Birth Rate	11
Growing Minority Enrollments	12
Legacy of the Baby Boom	13
Demographic Shifts	14
Transformation to an Information-Based Society	14
Changing Sex Roles	16
Increasing Narcissism	17
The Rapid Rate of Change	18
Summary	19
The Changing Political Terrain: Trends Affecting Higher Education	**21**
The Increasing Politicization of Higher Education	21
Accountability to the State	22
Federal Accountability	23
Judicial Influence	23
Changing Financial Conditions	25
Concern for Quality	26
Summary	27
Changing Student Clienteles	**29**
Changing Student Types	29
Changing Student Characteristics	36
Changing Institutional Strategies	**41**
Comprehensive Planning	43
Effective Information Systems	44
Enrollment Management	45
Recruitment	47
Retention	48
Preventive Law	50
Increasing Private Support	51
Changing Relationship of Business and Colleges	53
Management of Resources	54
Internal Accountability	55
Summary	56

The Integrator: A New Role Explained   **57**
Two Opposing Motivations   59
Moving Student Affairs into the Mainstream   60
Integration of Goals   62
Integration of Faculty and Student Affairs Efforts   66
Evolving Consumer Orientation   67
Developing a Greater External Focus   70
Summary   71

**Implications for Programs, Services, and
  Professional Skills**   **73**
New Skills for Professionals   73
Implications for Programs and Services   83
Summary   87

Educating Student Personnel Professionals   **89**
Preparation Programs   89
Preparation for Administration and Management   91
Entry-level Competencies   93
A New Model for Professional Preparation   94
Continuing Professional Education   95
Summary   98

The Challenges of Student Development   **99**
A Theoretical Basis for the Profession   99
Adoption and Application of Theory   100
Incorporating Diverse Clienteles   101
Integration with Administrative Practice   102
A New Theory of Development   104
Summary   105

Conclusions and Recommendations   **107**

References   **113**

Index   **127**

FOREWORD

Not so long ago, the role of college student personnel professionals was clearly defined. Their primary function on campuses was to serve as the most tangible agent of the policy in loco parentis, meaning that their specific duties were to act as disciplinarians, moderators of student behavior, and upholders of moral and social values. This role fell to student personnel professionals as much out of disinterest by other faculty as their own initiative.

Conditions on campuses have changed. For the most part, the idea of in loco parentis does not exist. The function of disciplinarian, then as now, obscured the obvious: the chief concern of college student professionals is the effective development of students. Development may be defined to include the moral, spiritual, and personal enrichment of the students, easing the transition from adolescent to young adult. Recent research on the outcomes of education indicate that affective development (instilling of values, behavior modification, and ways of thinking) is just as important as cognitive development, and has a more lasting effect on the students. This development occurs both outside as well as within classrooms. Therefore, college student personnel administrators have the potential of having as much impact on the students as the faculty.

The role of student affairs in the 80s, as Peter Garland, program analyst in the Office of Higher Education for the Pennsylvania Department of Education, suggests, has gone beyond the traditional role of guardian. These professionals have moved from the periphery to the center of the institution, sometimes influencing even survival. The student personnel administrator role is closely related to both the quality of the undergraduate nonclassroom experience, and student perceptions of the institution. This is a vital role, for future students are more often influenced by word-of-mouth recommendations than any standard recruiting technique. As many schools recognize, alumni are the strongest marketing tool an institution can employ.

It is now realized that college student personnel administrators have a greater role to play in many areas of the institution. For example, in addition to recruitment, there is a relationship to retention. A student affairs professional can make a world of difference to a student struggling to cope with ambiguities of the undergraduate experience and thus help reduce the chance of a student leaving before graduation. Student personnel administrators are also taking an active role in setting policies and procedures to maintain the harmonious relationship between the student and the institution, thereby minimizing possible threats of litigation. These new practices suggest that a redefinition of the role of college student personnel administrators is underway, and that to a large extent, these professionals can determine its development. How they choose to operate may set the standard for future practitioners.

This report, the seventh in the 1985 ASHE-ERIC Higher Education Report series, serves two distinct functions. First, it offers a more accurate portrayal of the important role student personnel administrators play in the everyday dynamics of successful colleges and universities. Second, it examines the specific development and effect of programs on students. Besides these descriptive functions, the book also offers recommendations for a conscious assessment of student personnel administrators and their staff, and for hiring personnel with specific academic backgrounds that will insure quality staffing of an office that has become integral to all facets of the institution. Staffing the student affairs office with personnel cognizant of and trained in multiple roles will result in not only a more productive office but also greater development of students. For many institutions, this will have a long-term influence on the future dynamics of their institutions.

Jonathan D. Fife
Series Editor
Professor and Director
ERIC Clearinghouse on Higher Education
The George Washington University

ACKNOWLEDGMENTS

I am indebted to many for their assistance in the preparation of this report: to Bob Hendrickson, associate professor of higher education at Penn State, and Lee Upcraft, director of counseling and health services at Penn State, for their thoughtful guidance on early drafts; to Dick Stevens, executive director of NASPA, for his insights offered on later drafts; to William Toombs, director of the Center for the Study of Higher Education at Penn State, for the support, direct and indirect, that he and the center provided while I explored and drafted this report; to S. V. Martorana, who has guided and shaped my development as a scholar; to Sally Kelly and Janet Shank of the center for their nimble fingers and critical eyes; and to a certain word processing unit for being my constant and sympathetic companion during many long days and nights. Despite their invaluable assistance, the contents remain solely my responsibility.

In addition, I must recognize the distant but important contribution of Jack Morgan, now vice president for student affairs at Maryville College (St. Louis), for it was in his class on student development at the College of William and Mary that the seeds of this report first took root.

THE EVOLVING ROLE OF STUDENT AFFAIRS

American higher education has evolved to meet society's changing needs. Eighteenth century society needed educated clergymen and societal leaders; thus, colonial colleges provided a pious liberal curriculum for those few men who would become church and political leaders (Rudolph 1962). But a century later, society evolved from an agrarian to an industrial society that needed a wider variety of social, political, and business leaders and expanded technologies to facilitate industrialization. Institutions responded by educating students for a wider range of roles in society, most notably through land-grant institutions and state universities that conducted pure and applied research and sought to provide direct service to society.

The most recent period in the evolution of higher education has occurred as a result of a post–World War II society that places a high value on education, career development, and educational opportunity for all. Society's expectations for research and service have been enhanced through increased governmental support for research, technological application, and educational service programs and activities. Institutions, responding to society's needs, have increased the diversity of students, programs of study, and educational activities (Kerr 1971).

As institutions have responded to society's needs, so too has student affairs. In colonial colleges, the student affairs function (performed by faculty and tutors) contributed to the intellectual and moral development that was the goal of those institutions. In expanding institutions of the nineteenth century, the student affairs professional coordinated and advised a growing number of extracurricular programs and services that mirrored expanding enrollments, an increasingly professional faculty, and greater amounts of student freedom (Rudolph 1962). In this century, an increasingly sophisticated student affairs profession has attempted to promote individual development as an educational goal.

Institutions in this decade are changing as a result of several trends. First, *society is changing,* including a decreasing birth rate (Glenny 1980), increasing minority populations (Glenny 1980), the information society (Naisbitt 1982), and the legacy of the baby boom (Upcraft, Finney, and Garland 1984). Second, *the higher education enterprise is changing,* including increased accountability (Har-

---

pel 1975), the application of management strategies to higher education (Baldridge and Tierney 1979), and renewed attention to academic quality (Study Group 1984). And, finally, *students are changing,* including growing minority enrollments (Cross 1981b), increasing vocationalism, and students' changing characteristics, needs, and values (Astin 1984a; Levine 1980).

In response, institutions are launching new or enhanced efforts aimed at recruiting and retaining students, institutional marketing, private fund raising, resource management, and the like. In many of these efforts, the role of student affairs is central and critical.

Growing recognition of the importance of the contributions of student affairs in many of these efforts is leading to an increased recognition of the congruity between the goals of student affairs and those of the institution. Several southern California institutions, for example, concerned about growing student attrition, launched major, institutionwide efforts to improve retention. Central to those efforts was the leadership of student affairs in areas like student advising and counseling, residential programs, student activities, orientation, on-campus student employment, and programs for commuting students. As a result of the strategies formulated to curb attrition, several of the institutions—Harvey Mudd College, Pitzer College, Azusa Pacific University, and Scripps College—experienced dramatic improvement in their retention of students, while others—Chapman College, Mount St. Mary's College, and Loyola Marymount University—reported that if it were not for the efforts, enrollments might have suffered (Green 1983). Similarly, students were more satisfied with college, more integrated with others in the institution, and more involved in student development. The complementary goals of the institution and of student affairs were both achieved.

Student affairs efforts employed by these institutions were activities demonstrated to be effective in the promotion of student involvement and ultimately retention (Astin 1984b). *Student involvement* is defined as "the amount of physical and psychological energy that the student devotes to the academic experience," and it is a powerful contributor to increased retention, satisfaction with college, and achievement (p. 297). It would be hard to underestimate

the importance of student affairs in promoting and supporting students' involvement.

Thus, the goals of student affairs—particularly the goal
of student involvement—is recognized as critically important to a growing number of institutions. Responding to
changing societal needs, student affairs has assumed a
number of important roles in colleges and universities, and
the potential for increased importance of student affairs
calls for a rethinking of the role of student affairs. The role
of student affairs has evolved from disciplinarian to custodian to educator, and while each of these roles has characterized the major focus of the student affairs professional,
each incorporates previous roles. The role of student
affairs has grown by accretion, not substitution, toward an
increasingly complex set of duties and roles.

*The role of
student affairs
has grown by
accretion, not
substitution.*

Student affairs professionals are now performing integrating functions within the institution, integrating students' needs and traditional student affairs goals on the one
hand and the varied needs of institutions responding to
changing conditions on the other. Changes in society, in
higher education, and in students, and institutional responses in light of those changes, argue for a new major
focus for the student affairs role. The role of student affairs
is ready once again to evolve—into that of *institutional
integrator*. This role, which recognizes the contributions of
student affairs to the institution in a new light, calls for an
examination of student affairs programs and services and
the skills professionals need. Perhaps most important, it
places demands on the preparation and continuing professional education of student affairs staff.

The Disciplinarian
The tutors responsible for student affairs in the colonial
colleges acted as guardians of moral development to monitor students' behavior. *In loco parentis,* which guided the
relationship between the student and the institution until
recent years, is rooted in this concern for the moral development of young students. College officials, acting in the
place of parents, monitored students' social and moral
development, which often entailed punishing students for
violations of any of hundreds of rules (Rudolph 1962). The
student affairs portion of their work consisted of "a persis-
tent emphasis on extracurricular religion, and also a con-

siderable snooping into the personal lives of the student"
(Cowley 1949, p. 20).

The goal of education in the colonial and pre–Civil War
period was to develop in the young student a disciplined
mind and soul; put another way, the goal of institutions
was the development of a proper morality befitting an educated man. As a result, the academic and student affairs
function remained complementary goals of the faculty
(Rudolph 1962).

This period of student discipline, regarded as *the*
approach to student affairs, began to change with the
increasing numbers of students and the growing complexity
of colleges. The notion that certain members of the college
community would be responsible for monitoring students'
behavior and student discipline would remain with student
affairs to this day, however.

The Custodian
The rise of the American university, incorporating the evolution of the academic profession and the diversification of
institutional mission, led to the establishment and expansion
of the student services profession. Perhaps the most influential of these trends was the increasing specialization of the
faculty. Tired of his responsibilities for student discipline,
enlivened by opportunities to conduct research and pursue
scholarship, the academic man of the late 1800s sought to rid
himself of the more onerous responsibilities associated with
student life. The birth of the student affairs profession is usually marked by the appointment of the first personnel dean at
Harvard in 1870 to handle student discipline. His appointment was to take the burden of student discipline off the
shoulders of the newly appointed president, Charles William
Eliot, who sought to free his time and that of the faculty for
pursuit of research and scholarship (Fenske 1980). Most universities and many colleges soon adopted the appointment of
a student personnel officer.

Increasing specialization and complexity characterized
expanding colleges and universities. Likewise, activities in
the extracurriculum proliferated in the post–Civil War
period. Seeking more stimulation than the classroom experience could provide, students became involved in Greek
letter societies, intercollegiate athletics, student publications, and literary and debating societies (Rudolph 1962).

As a response to the growing number of activities in student life, institutions began to employ student services administrators to oversee and advise the activities that soon came to be an important part of the collegiate experience.

Through much of this period, student personnel staff retained custodial responsibility over students' behavior while increasing their responsibility in an ever-larger number of student activities. In addition, a number of student-related functions, including registration, advising, and counseling, became the province of student affairs staff (Cowley 1949).

The Educator
The post–World War I expansion of the student personnel movement occurred as a result of the acceptance of mental testing and counseling employed on a large scale by the Army during the war (Brubacher and Rudy 1976). The use of counseling and testing to help the individual gained credibility and was adopted on college and university campuses. The growth of counseling offered student affairs staff a greater degree of professionalism. Furthermore, the development and application of new psychological and pedagogical theories supported the need for the student personnel function. The higher education community was coming to accept the notion that noncognitive needs were important to the development of college students. Student health services, career placement, and intramural and intercollegiate athletics became part of an expanding and diversifying student affairs function on many college and university campuses (Brubacher and Rudy 1976).

Recovering from setbacks as a result of the depression, the student affairs profession prospered in the period preceding and just following World War II, a period that has been referred to as a "golden age" for the profession (Deegan 1981). These years saw an increase in the identity, the emphasis, and the sophistication of student affairs functions. Publications by the American Council on Education describing college student personnel work sharpened the philosophical basis of the profession (ACE 1938; Williamson 1949). These statements emphasized the underlying spirit of the work, "the personnel point of view," and were based on three assumptions:

1. Individual differences are anticipated, and every student is recognized as unique.
2. Each individual is to be treated as a functioning whole.
3. The individual's current drives, interests, and needs are to be accepted as the most significant factor in developing a personnel program appropriate for any particular campus (Deegan 1981, p. 2).

The 1960s and 1970s were special for the student personnel profession. Continued expansion of higher education resulted in increased numbers of professionals with specialized abilities. Student affairs was called upon to provide a wider array of services in admissions, registration and records, financial aid, housing and food services, student activities, personal and academic counseling, orientation, and special services to a growing student body.

It was also a period of student unrest, however, the aftermath of which proved to be a significant philosophical loss for the profession. *In loco parentis,* which institutions employed to guide their relations with students, was one of the many casualties of the period, along with the authority structures it created. Student personnel staff were caught in the awkward position of having to react to rapid changes without a guiding philosophy.

As a result, an increasingly diverse and complex profession sought to reestablish its theoretical and operational base and to embrace a philosophy to guide its efforts within the institution. Out of this concern, the Tomorrow's Higher Education Project of the American College Personnel Association emerged as an effort to define the mission and role of student affairs; a result was the commitment to student development (the theories of human development applied to postsecondary education) as a guiding philosophy, if not theory, and the continued attempt to ensure that the development of the whole person was an institutional priority.

To meet the goal of student development, a model comprised of six major components was proposed—goal setting, assessment, instruction, consultation, management, and evaluation. Through these components, student development specialists sought to anticipate change, to better coordinate academic and student affairs programs, and to develop a more comprehensive educational dimension to the student affairs profession (Miller and Prince 1977). The student personnel professional sought to become more than a disciplinarian of student conduct or a custodian of student services; he sought instead to become a human services professional responsible for shaping the development of students and student groups within the institutional setting.

The Role of Student Affairs Today
The history of student affairs has been characterized by increasing specialization and complexity. The student affairs function, once the responsibility of faculty, has increasingly fallen to nonacademic professionals, and it is typically viewed as an academic support function and dismissed as peripheral (McConnell 1970). But changing conditions in society, students, and higher education demand new responses from institutions, and the involvement of student affairs in those responses is increasingly important. This change comes largely as a result of increasingly complementary institutional and student affairs goals in the recruitment and retention of students, their placement in careers after graduation, and the integration and involvement of diverse student clienteles. Student affairs professionals have the opportunity to take the lead in achieving institutional goals and, in so doing, integrating professional goals (the development of students) with institutional goals (organizational development). Some of them are doing so already:

1. At several private institutions in California, student affairs leaders were instrumental in improving student retention.
2. At the University of Maryland, a course for adult students addresses social and emotional needs in addition to cognitive needs.
3. The parents' association at Pennsylvania State University was initiated to enhance parents' involvement in student development as well as to develop fundraising strategies designed for the group.

The idea that student affairs professionals can serve an integrating function within the institution is not new. In the future, if it is to remain vital, the student personnel field must contribute to the institution as a whole and not solely to student development:

If the developmental model emerged in part to supply a positive and less reactive approach to student life, then we must now move to the next step to incorporate a positive approach to institutional life and to respond positively to the issues facing our institutions (Smith 1982, p. 57).

The term "integrator" was suggested in 1971 as the name for the new and potential role of student affairs (Silverman 1971). The student affairs organization shares the orientation of the three major campus groups—faculty, students, and administrators—and its position on the borders of these groups may be its greatest strength:

Our uniqueness as student personnel workers rests on our ability to fashion significant educational environments, using the resources, values, norms, and opportunities of the variety of constituencies on our campuses. To the extent that we are successful in our innovative work, we will be respected, not because of position, but as a result of the impacts we have on campus life. Truly, student personnel workers have the opportunities to be central figures for campus improvement in an era when resources must be perceived as newly combined rather than as new (Silverman 1980, p. 12).

As integrators, student affairs professionals will define their priorities and goals in terms of those of the institution in addition to those of the student. They will serve both institution and student as *advocate* and *advisor*. The student affairs professional has typically sought to integrate institutional goals and the goals of the profession in serving students, but the importance of those efforts is increasingly recognized with attention to new conditions. Integrating student and institutional needs, the student affairs professional will serve in a number of capacities not envisioned in the "traditional" student affairs role.

The student affairs professional—today and in the future—must integrate the traditional student affairs roles of disciplinarian, custodian, and student development educator with the roles of environmental scanner, market analyst, legal advisor, development officer, and manager. And as an integrator, the student affairs professional must focus attention on both students' needs and the institution's needs and seek to match efforts to satisfy both sets of needs. The student affairs function as an integrating one will be increasingly important to the identification and achievement of institutional goals.

A CHANGING SOCIETY

Higher education is constantly evolving, but changes in the
past 15 years have been particularly noteworthy and are
demanding responses from higher education. More specifically, demographic changes affecting enrollments are
changing the outlooks and goals of many institutions; financial limitations as a result of leveling or decreasing enrollments and increasing accountability of public funds are
eroding the flexibility of institutions to meet changing conditions; and increased participation in postsecondary education by women, blacks, Hispanics, adults, the handicapped, and academically underprepared students is
changing students' needs and demands to which institutions must respond.

Society is not static; it changes over time and the institutions serving society similarly change over time. Colleges
and universities are facing a number of significant societal
changes that challenge their mission, curricula, the needs
of students, and methods of operation. Among the changes
that society and institutions must face are a decline in the
birth rate, growing minority enrollments, the legacy of the
baby boom, demographic shifts, an evolving information
society and economy, changing sex roles, and growing evidence of narcissism of individuals and groups.

A Declining Birth Rate

After World War II, the number of births in the United
States increased dramatically to 4.3 million at its peak in
1957. Since that peak, commonly referred to as the baby
boom, the birth rate has declined steadily, and with it has
come a similar decrease in the number of students of traditional college age (18 to 24 years old). Despite the fact that
the birth rate has recently begun to increase slightly, no
rapid increase in the birth rate is expected between now
and the end of the century (Glenny 1980).

A declining birth rate is particularly serious for higher
education as it translates into a decline in the number of
students of traditional college age, the group that has been
the historical mainstay of college enrollments. While
numerous institutions by design or necessity are attracting
more older students, the traditional age group remains
important for most institutions. A discussion of retrenchment in the 1980s concluded that declining birth rates and a

---

related decline in the number of 18-year-old student enrollments are major reasons for a reduction in the budget base
of many institutions (Mortimer and Tierney 1979).

Various researchers (Carnegie Council 1980; Centra 1980)
have attempted to project enrollments in higher education
incorporating birth rate, college attendance trends, and social
and economic factors. Despite a recognition of the increasing
enrollment of nontraditional students in colleges and universities, most projections claim that enrollments will decrease.
Although enrollments have not declined as projected for the
early 1980s, much of the decline in traditional age students is
still ahead (O'Keefe 1985). As a result of concerns over
enrollments, institutions have become more aggressive and
competitive in recruiting and more active in retaining students. The development of marketing plans and retention
strategies is becoming critical to institutions seeking to
address possible shortfalls in enrollment. Institutionwide
efforts to attract and retain students call for significant
involvement by student affairs, involvement that will
enhance the role of student affairs in institutions (Baldridge,
Kemerer, and Green 1982).

Growing Minority Enrollments
Declining birth rates do not tell the complete story of the
changing demographics of higher education. If birth rates
are disaggregated by race or ethnic origin, a more complex
picture emerges. The birth rates among whites, blacks, and
Hispanics are substantially different; they are much higher
for blacks and Hispanics than for whites (Glenny 1980;
Hodgkinson 1984).

While the proportional increases in minority populations
may not be as great in the future as they have been in the
past 15 years, the effects of that period will have implications for higher education in the near future. In 1977, for
instance, 29 percent of whites, 39 percent of blacks, and 42
percent of Hispanics were under 18 (Glenny 1980). As a
result, increasing numbers of blacks and Hispanics are
entering the traditional college-age cohort each year.

As these minority groups become more actively
recruited to higher education, institutions will be under
pressure to respond to the different learning styles, diverse
social and emotional needs, and educational expectations

of many of these new participants. In recognition of these needs and expectations, many institutions are attempting to provide more flexible financial aid programs, appropriate personal and academic counseling, enhanced career planning and placement activities, and effective academic support services. As the provider of many of these services, student affairs organizations are called upon to modify existing models and practices to meet the needs of new student clienteles.

Legacy of the Baby Boom

Adjusting to a lower birth rate is but one of the adjustments that society must make to the postwar baby boom generation. The effects on society brought about by a baby boom in the 1950s and early 1960s, followed by an equally precipitous decline in birth rate in the late 1960s and early 1970s, are difficult to overestimate. The increasing number of births in the 1950s and 1960s was instrumental in fostering a "youth culture" in society, fueling the creation and expansion of new industries and services directed at the needs and wants of that age group and causing the massive mobilization of the nation to educate its youth through the college years (Jones 1980). But a decline in the birth rate carries with it similarly important implications for society. As a society, we are aging. In the next 20 years, a middle-aged society will be emerging that will capture the attention—if not the policy directions—of society, suggesting the decreasing importance of education (Rhatigan 1979).

The first wave of baby boomers (those born between 1946 and 1954) has enjoyed the benefits of an expanding society, including ready career advancement and mobility, business opportunities, and the fulfillment of the American Dream (two cars, a house in the suburbs, and so on). Those born since the mid-1950s, however, are subject to a changing economy, increased competition for careers, and diminished expectations (Upcraft, Finney, and Garland 1984). Competition for middle-management jobs (the so-called "promotion squeeze") may become increasingly fierce. Entering an era of diminishing expectations, perhaps for the first time in recent history, the outlook and energy of society as well as of college students is changing.

A recent article on job prospects for college graduates paints a dreary picture for college graduates in the 1980s

Institutionwide efforts to attract and retain students call for significant involvement by student affairs.

(Rumberger 1984). Educational attainment will continue to increase among workers, but, while college graduates will continue to hold a competitive advantage in the labor market, an increasing number will accept positions not commensurate with their level of training.

Recognition of the legacy of the baby boom is altering students' expectations of college, and career pressures are growing for members of the current student generation. Students' aspirations may be unrealistic, and student affairs professionals, in counseling students, will need to address the adjustment to diminished expectations or find alternate routes to the fulfillment of expectations.

Demographic Shifts

Census maps and figures prepared by the Bureau of the Census validate a commonly perceived trend: that the American population is moving out of the industrialized Northeast and Upper Midwest to the sun belt that stretches from California to Florida. Industries, including professional and service industries, are following a similar trend (Hodgkinson 1984).

As a result of the movement to the sun belt, society in general, individual states, and regions have changed profoundly. As the population, particularly the younger population, moves south, the aging society it leaves behind places increased pressure on state economies damaged by a mobile job market and shrinking tax bases. Older persons and displaced workers place increased demands on states for social services. As a result, educational institutions must compete more with other state agencies and services for funds, and they must increasingly justify their costs in terms of benefits to society. Changing social priorities and the resultant accountability for limited funds place pressures on institutions to manage resources more effectively and may hamper efforts made to respond to changing conditions. Likewise, student affairs divisions have found themselves increasingly accountable for the same or diminished resources (Harpel 1975; Silverman 1980).

Transformation to an Information-Based Society

It is evident that we no longer dominate the world's economic order as we once did. Other nations are challenging our once unshakable position as the greatest industrialized nation in the world. The traditional anchors of our industrial might—steel, autos, and other heavy industries—are suffering from stiff competition overseas. At a time when our large industrial corporations are in decline and we turn to other countries for our steel, cars, and consumer products, however, we are expanding our information-based industries and services. While our dependence on industrial production is waning, our reliance upon information and its processing is growing. The process represents a profound change in our economic system.

More of us than ever are working in information-related occupations. In 1950, for example, only 17 percent of the workforce was employed in jobs where information was the product. Today, more than 60 percent of us work in information-related occupations as lawyers, clerks, secretaries, managers, programmers, teachers, technicians, and the like, and fewer than 13 percent of us are now engaged in industrial production (Naisbitt 1982).

The symbol of the new information age, the computer, is leading to profound changes in the way we work, the way we learn, and the ways in which we communicate and relate to one another. Computer technology is revamping industrial production, the education of our youth, and the forms in which we record and interpret ourselves and our society. Traditional jobs and careers become obsolete or redirected, while others are created overnight. The result is pressure to reeducate and retrain significant portions of our workforce each year.

Understanding this situation, one must acknowledge the difficulty of choosing a marketable career in such a rapidly changing environment. Pressures to become computer-literate and to prepare for high-technology careers are growing, but no one guarantees that career preparation will last a lifetime. Preparing students to become lifelong learners will increasingly be a challenge of most institutions. This goal is made more difficult because of immediate pressures for the provision of education for employment upon graduation. Opportunities and challenges arise from this scenario for student affairs to counsel and advise students on careers and major choices, to interpret the changing world of work, and to provide leadership in placement.

In reeducation and retraining activities, institutions are facing greater challenges from other organizations and

industries for the provision of educational services. Student affairs programs and services—to the extent that they distinguish the educational efforts of colleges and universities—will become increasingly important to institutions' success in meeting competition from other educational providers.

Changing Sex Roles

Traditional role expectations for men and women are changing today, as are distinctions between what is expected "male" and "female" behavior. For women in particular, opportunities have increased for participation in fields and careers not open to them even a generation ago. Labor-saving devices in the home have decreased the amount of time necessary for family care, birth control has given women control over when and whether they will bear children, and the women's movement has given focus to and support for women who become more involved in education and careers once virtually closed to women (Cross 1981a).

Increasing numbers of women are entering such male-dominated fields as engineering, business, applied technologies, and the pure sciences (Astin and others 1984). Increasingly, women are becoming a substantial minority in high-prestige professions such as medicine, dentistry, and the law.

As women participate more fully in society, their traditional roles are changing; women in nontraditional careers view their role choices as less constrained. As women's sex roles become less traditional, men too become able to choose from a wider range of behaviors. Both men and women increasingly make alternative choices and set different priorities for careers, marriage, and children, with each taking a greater responsibility for the decisions (Upcraft, Finney, and Garland 1984).

The polarizations between males and females in the family are being transcended, and a growing synergy between male and female roles is becoming apparent (Friedan 1981). It occurs as more men and women attempt to understand themselves and others and the opportunities that are available to both. Careers outside of the home increase options in sex roles, and the two-paycheck couple may be an important vehicle for changing sex roles. While dual careers offer increased opportunities for both men and women in the home and in the workplace, however, so too do they increase confusion about roles (Hester and Dickerson 1982).

All these trends have important implications for student affairs. With more women enrolled in a wider variety of majors, preparing to assume new and different roles, the need for academic and personal support services has increased. Support services become even more important with the realization that, even as opportunities exist for new roles, most women experience traditional socialization and lifestyle patterns (Hester and Dickerson 1982). Preparing men and women to be able to work together is a new challenge for student development (Abrams 1981).

Increasing Narcissism
Our society is moving from a period of concern about social issues to a primary focus on personal issues. We have been described as living in an age of the "new narcissism" (Lasch 1978), typified by "me-ism" (Levine 1980), while our college students are described as the "now" or "me" generation (Suchinsky 1982). We are increasingly self-concerned and self-directed, participating in a period of "individual ascendancy" that emphasizes hedonism and the primacy of duty to the self, in contrast to a period of "community ascendancy" that emphasizes asceticism and the importance of duty to others (Levine 1980). Consider, for example, that 91 percent of students today hold high hopes for themselves, while only 41 percent are similarly optimistic about society (Levine 1980).

Examples of societal narcissism abound (Suchinsky 1982). We are obsessively concerned about our appearance, our success, and our possessions. Our interpersonal relationships are often transitory and trivial, and we are more willing to sacrifice relationships with others in competing for financial security and professional advancement (Upcraft, Finney, and Garland 1984). Growing narcissism means we are less willing to sacrifice personal fulfillment for the benefit of our spouse, our children, and our friends (Levine 1980).

In light of these societal trends, it is perhaps understandable that students have become more concerned about themselves, their success, and other personal issues. Narcissistic students have important implications for institutions and student affairs organizations. Students often view extracurricular activities as an opportunity to add depth instead of breadth to their academic program. Narcissistic students may be more interested in health and fitness and more willing to assert their personal rights. Student affairs professionals must therefore reorganize efforts to respond to the needs and problems of self-concerned students (Suchinsky 1982).

The Rapid Rate of Change

Although change is inevitable, it may be occurring so fast that it is beyond our comprehension. Change is occurring so rapidly that often little time is available to understand it or even to react before things have changed again. This rapid rate of change affects our society in several ways. First, the rate of change is getting faster. The delay between a technological idea and its application is rapidly decreasing, allowing us less time to adjust to technological change (Naisbitt 1982). This increasing rate of change and growing technological complexity place increased stress on society and individuals (Chickering and associates 1981; Toffler 1970).

Second, rapid change calls for more insightful, adaptable generalists who can understand a complex world rather than narrowly trained specialists. Third, rapid change demands that we rethink the notion of a discrete educational period followed by the pursuit of a career. Education and work should no longer be viewed as a linear relationship, as opportunities and demands for both become more blended (Cross 1981a, 1981b). A changing economic base demands new skills and careers, and the route to them is often through education and training.

Fourth, rapid change demands that we look to the future for guidance rather than to the past in our efforts to understand and anticipate it. Our time focus and the focus of understanding it implies must change from the past to the future (Naisbitt 1982).

Fifth, rapid change challenges our values. At a time when we must look to the future, our values are rooted in the past. The development of values is typically one of the educational objectives of most institutions, even though colleges and universities often do very little to promote the exploration and development of values (Bok 1976).

Finally, a rapidly changing world is also a more interdependent world. Global issues like famine, energy, nuclear war, and terrorism bring events closer to home each year, and dealing with them adds to our stress.

The changes in society that place pressures on institutions to respond are each enhanced by the rapid rate of change. As a result, responses are demanded of institutions and student affairs organizations. Among the effects on student affairs organizations are pressures to help students develop and adapt value systems that accommodate future changes, to develop intellectual and emotional skills to cope with the explosion of knowledge, and to prepare for lifelong learning.

Summary

Societal change is constant and varied, and it directly and indirectly places pressure on institutions to adapt. Demographic trends, economic evolution, evolving sex roles, narcissism, and even the increasing rate of change itself demand timely and dynamic responses by institutions.

Among the responses that institutions are making are those in which student affairs has the potential for leadership or significant participation. They include the provision of new or enhanced support services for diverse student clienteles, participation in the management of enrollments, attention to students' changing expectations and the development of values, enhanced career planning and placement activities, and attention to changing sex roles and their implications for students. To the extent that student affairs professionals are able to take leadership in these areas and contribute meaningfully to students and to the institution itself, their role within the institution will be enhanced and strengthened. Their role will be to ensure that the goals of the student affairs profession will become more integrated with those of the institution.

THE CHANGING POLITICAL TERRAIN:
Trends Affecting Higher Education

In addition to changes demanded by societal forces, other more direct forces place pressure on higher education to reexamine its relationship with society, its mission and purpose, and its efforts in relation to them. Chief among these trends is the changing political terrain for higher education, including accountability to state legislatures, state and federal agencies, and state and federal courts; changing relationships with business and industry; and increased competition for funds and students. These changes affect institutions' missions, priorities, programs, and services, and they call for responses by student affairs.

That institutions of higher education are facing increased demands from external sources is a fact most educators know all too well. Increasingly, institutions are subject to the demands of Congress, legislatures, state and federal agencies, and the courts. Once largely neglected by these authorities, colleges and universities are finding their day-to-day relationships with external sources increasingly complex. This phenomenon is a result of the increasing politicization of higher education, increasing oversight by legislatures and state and federal agencies, and increased attention by courts at all levels.

The Increasing Politicization of Higher Education
Increased accountability to state and federal governments is just one factor in the increasing politicization of higher education. The notions that education and politics do not mix and that educational decisions should be separate from political decisions have been carefully nurtured but failing myths. While educators cultivated the notion that education functioned as a nonpartisan, closed system apart from the larger political system (Iannaccone 1967), external pressures for change were reduced and even eliminated in some cases (Blocker, Bender, and Martorana 1975).

Today, however, educators increasingly recognize the politics of education policy, largely because of the increased competition for less state and federal money (Rosenthal and Fuhrman 1981). Education policy making has evolved from a closed system with few participants to one in which decision making has become more open, pluralistic, and politicized (Murphy 1980). At the same time, policy making for education at all levels has become more centralized at the state level (Millard 1976). Few decisions within the institution are made without attention to their political implications.

Accountability to the State

Despite the existence of public policies affecting higher education, state agencies and legislatures were generally unconcerned about accountability until recently. State involvement with private institutions was even less extensive. But such is not the case in the 1980s.

State governing and coordinating structures for higher education have grown in size and power in recent years (Berdahl 1971; Millard 1976). The formulation of federally sponsored planning commissions in most states in the 1970s brought private institutions into state planning and coordinating activities (Millard 1976). Similarly, the amount of legislation in recent years affecting higher education has increased considerably; higher education is subject to policies intended for all state agencies as well as legislation targeted solely for higher education (Martorana and Corbett 1983).

States are increasingly concerned that monies for higher education are expended with state policy priorities in mind. As a result, it is not unusual today to find that a public college or university will be accountable, to varying degrees, to the state coordinating or governing board, to the departments of purchasing, personnel, computer and management information systems, finance, and occupational safety, and to the civil rights commission. In addition, an institution typically has general and special responsibilities to the state legislature. The picture for private institutions is different, but a similar trend emerges if the institution receives state funds.

Accountability affects all of an institution's programs and activities, including student affairs. Increased attention to compliance with state statutes and rules affects both the administration of student affairs and the programs and services offered. Student affairs organizations in public institutions are accountable to various state agencies for their administration and programs, but more important, accountability typically translates into information about costs and outcome for various efforts. It is in this area that student affairs is most vulnerable. Support for student affairs programs has long been justified on humanitarian grounds rather than on tangible measures of cost and outcome, and as a result, principles of accountability and current resource management models like those developed by the National Center for Higher Education Management Systems should be translated into useful models for the profession (Harpel 1975).

Federal Accountability

Accountability to the federal government occurs as a result of federal legislation, regulations issued by federal agencies and commissions, and attention by the courts. Federal legislation and regulations governing the activities of institutions have increased at an alarming rate, according to most university administrators; for most institutions, compliance is a major activity. In general, institutions are held accountable for the guarantee of equal opportunity and access, affirmative action, administrative due process, and constitutional rights. By accepting federal funds, directly through sponsored research and other federal programs and indirectly as a result of enrolling students receiving federal financial aid, both public and private institutions are required to comply with federal policies and reporting requirements. Compliance with federal regulations costs time and money, but perhaps most important, it shapes institutional policy and practice.

Attention to federal policy directed at affirmative action, equal opportunity, and due process shapes admissions and financial aid policies and student discipline. As a result, student affairs organizations are increasingly concerned with the interpretation of federal policies, making practices more formal, regularized, and expensive. Similarly, student affairs leaders must participate in the institutional process that integrates institutional priorities, rights, and students' responsibilities in their efforts.

Judicial Influence

Just as the influence of Congress, state legislatures, and various federal and state agencies has grown, so too has the influence of the courts on higher education. Historically, American courts have exercised academic deference in matters where academic judgments have been deemed most important. The result in most cases was little judicial influence over academic institutions. Academic deference,

States are increasingly concerned that monies for higher education are expended with state policy priorities in mind.

despite its pervasiveness, was largely an informal practice (Edwards and Nordin 1979).

Court intervention in academic issues, however, has increased in recent years for a number of reasons, among them increasing familiarity with the legal process, growing concern for civil rights, increased governmental regulations, and increased reliance on the courts for redress of grievances by individuals and groups (Brubacher 1971; Edwards and Nordin 1979). The volume of litigation and the amount of effort expended by institutional administrators on legal matters has increased greatly in the past few years (Kaplan 1978).

While court intervention has increased in recent years, it has been selective. Courts have been most concerned with the constitutional rights of individuals and contractual obligations between individuals and institutions. As a result, judicial activity in the areas of discrimination, due process, and contracts has increased. On the other hand, in areas where academic judgment is best left alone—in determining admission standards, curricula, and faculty tenure, for example—academic deference is still exercised so long as individual rights and fairness are ensured (Kaplan 1978).

Judicial decisions affect all areas of the institution, but they are most likely to affect student affairs in the areas of constitutional and contractual rights that shape the student/institutional relationship. In a number of recent cases, jurists have sought to define the relationship between the student and the institution and the rights of each in that relationship. Much of the increased caseload involving higher education in the 1960s was brought by students challenging *in loco parentis* and lack of due process in institutional actions. In addition, the federal government has been active in seeking judicial redress for discrimination by institutions. Today, students are turning to litigation to ensure their rights as consumers in the educational enterprise (Levine 1980; Stark and associates 1977) in addition to securing their civil rights.

Cases of interest to student affairs professionals tend to center in four areas:

1. The infringement of individual rights in the admissions process, in academic evaluation, and in other

actions taken by the institution where administrative
due process is not adhered to
2. Contractual rights between students and institutions
   in cases involving the awarding of credits and degrees, admissions policy, financial aid, and an institution's auxiliary operations
3. Student discipline systems
4. Numerous cases concerning student organizations
   (Kaplan 1978).

Issues in these cases typically focus on the rights of students to organize and to have access to institutional funds
and facilities, as well as on nondiscrimination in member-
ship. In addition, institutions' and administrators' liability
for the actions of organizations sanctioned by the institution has become the focus in recent cases (Kaplan 1978).

For these reasons, institutions are increasingly concerned about their legal position. Student affairs organizations, because of their many functions, are becoming
increasingly aware of legal issues in their relationships with
students and organizations vis-à-vis due process, discrimination, contractual rights and obligations, and liability in
student activities. Student affairs professionals are becoming more aware of the legal ramifications of their actions.
Knowledge of legal issues in these matters must be further
integrated with institutional practice and students' needs in
formulating responses.

Changing Financial Conditions

The dire financial condition of colleges and universities has
been discussed often in the past 15 years. The "golden
age" of the 1960s has been replaced by the "new depression" of the 1970s, 1980s, and beyond. Despite the fact
that projected enrollment declines have been offset by
increased enrollments of nontraditional students and that
financial support for most institutions has been increasing
(according to the annual reports on funding submitted by
M. M. Chambers), most institutions remain concerned
about enrollments and the public accountability of funds.

Recent years have seen an increase in the accountability
that state and federal governments have retained over
much of their funds, and increased accountability has

caused a loss of discretionary authority over funds (Kramer 1980). Most institutions will likely face decreasing discretionary funds, which will severely hamper institutions' efforts to meet changing conditions (Carnegie Council 1980; Kramer 1980).

Internal reallocations and reductions are typically part of the budget and planning process as institutions seek to reduce or control expenditures (Mortimer and Tierney 1979), and changing financial conditions are often felt most sharply in student affairs divisions (Deegan 1981; Harpel 1975). With reduced budgets and demands for new efforts, student affairs organizations, much like the institutions of which they are a part, must more carefully manage their resources.

Concern for Quality

Not all of the forces bearing on higher education deal with legal and financial relationships; lately growing attention has been focused on the improvement of quality in higher education (Bennett 1984; National Commission 1983; Study Group 1984). Each report suggests ways that institutions can improve the quality of education they offer. One common theme is the importance placed on students' involvement in the academic experience. While recommendations are specified for the range and types of skills to be acquired and the content areas to be mastered, the involvement of faculty, students, and administrators in the learning experience is emphasized as the critical factor in the achievement of quality.

The recommendations of these reports represent a challenge to American higher education just as important as legal and financial challenges. Perhaps more than other trends, concern for the improvement of academic quality provides special opportunities for the student affairs profession. *Involvement in Learning* (Study Group 1984) suggests a strong role for student affairs in the enhancement of involvement and, ultimately, the improvement of quality in the undergraduate experience. Several of the report's recommendations call directly for a response by student affairs:

- All colleges should offer a systematic program of guidance and advisement that involves students from matriculation through graduation. Student affairs personnel, peer counselors, faculty, and administrators should all participate in this system on a continuing basis (p. 31).

- Every institution of higher education should strive to create learning communities organized around specific intellectual themes or tasks (p. 33).
- Academic and student service administrators should provide adequate fiscal support, space, and recognition to existing cocurricular programs and activities to make the most of students' involvement. Every attempt should be made to include part-time and commuter students in such programs and activities (p. 35).

Summary

While institutions are under pressure to adapt to societal change, changes in higher education are demanding responses by institutions. The world of postsecondary education has changed: Institutions have become more accountable to a variety of state, federal, and local agencies; state and federal courts are selectively eroding academic discretion in relationships between students and institutions; and a degree of financial uncertainty characterizes the future of many institutions. These changes are demanding institutional responses that in turn alter the goals and priorities of institutions.

In large measure, these changes lead to changes in the goals, priorities, programs, and services of student affairs organizations, and these changes have implications for student affairs: (1) increased attention to the political implications of policies and programs; (2) increased accountability to the state in administrative practices and in the allocation and expenditure of funds; (3) increased accountability to the federal government in practices concerning student rights; (4) increased attention to the rights of students and the legal process; (5) changing financial conditions that are eroding funds and flexibility for all institutional units; and (6) new opportunities to contribute to the quality of the educational experience. These implications suggest a new role for student affairs that is at once both expanded and more central, a role in which student affairs serves not just students, but faculty and the institution at large. It is a role that calls for the integration of student, faculty, and institutional needs in a way not previously envisioned.

CHANGING STUDENT CLIENTELES

Another area of significant change affecting the role of student affairs is that of the college student. Attention to the needs of the traditional college student—18 to 24 years old, middle-class, white—that has guided student affairs efforts must be expanded as a result of changes in the student body. Today more women, minority, older, part-time, disabled, and underprepared students attend college. And these nontraditional students differ from traditional students: They generally have multiple commitments, are not campus-focused, and prefer informal learning situations (Hughes 1983). They bring with them different values, learning styles, expectations for career and lifestyle, educational expectations and motivations, and personal developmental needs. Furthermore, the goals and values of traditional students are different from those of their predecessors (Astin and others 1984).

The diversity of today's students and their needs is challenging institutional traditions and student affairs professionals, who must address these changing student types and characteristics and their integration with the institution's priorities. That integration holds great promise for the student affairs profession.

Changing Student Types
The traditional student has typically been defined as white, middle-class, 18 to 24 years old, and adequately prepared for college-level academic work. With growing numbers of students not fitting this description, however, the "traditional" student is fast becoming a minority in higher education. Several different trends in enrollment suggest that the makeup of college students is changing.

Women
Women are no longer a minority in postsecondary education. Since 1979, women have outnumbered men in the total enrollment of colleges and universities. More important, more young women are interested in higher paying, higher prestige careers that demand a college education (Carnegie Council 1980). Yet only recently have institutions begun to address the special needs of women.

Increased participation by women in higher education, however, has created new problems. Women often lack role models in male-dominated fields and are often the targets of discrimination and sexual harassment. While expectations about sex roles are changing, women (particularly those in nontraditional fields) find it difficult to resolve demands made by their chosen careers and traditional socialization (Hester and Dickerson 1982).

In addition to the increasing number of women in the traditional college age group, significant numbers of older women are returning to college. Because the reasons for returning are varied, the special needs of older women are similarly diverse. These older women differ from traditional students in their needs for flexible scheduling, daycare services, lifestyle and vocational counseling, assertiveness training, assistance when discriminated against and harassed, flexible financial aid, and opportunities for role models, support groups, and family counseling (Wheaton and Robinson 1983). Despite the high motivation that characterizes returning women, these women often feel inadequate and threatened upon reentering the academic setting, particularly in the possession of specific competencies (Vasquez and Chavez 1980). The learning styles of returning women differ from those of traditional students, and institutions must address those differences (Cross 1981a).

Minorities
An increasing number of minorities, including blacks, Hispanics, and native Americans, are participating in higher education. The college-going rate of 18- to 24-year-old blacks will soon equal that of whites (Carnegie Council 1980). For black students, equal opportunity policies, affirmative action programs, and active recruitment contribute to increasing attendance. Further, black students recognize that opportunities and increased income are significantly improved by college attendance (Rumberger 1984). Recent reports, however, suggest that participation by black students has not increased as expected as a result of changing federal aid policies (Ostar 1985), which does not diminish the importance of blacks and other minority students on most campuses.

Hispanic students are likewise beginning to increase their participation in postsecondary education, despite a lower high school completion rate than either blacks or whites (Glenny 1980). And in several states, increasing numbers of native Americans are participating in postsecondary education.

While minority student groups differ, it can be generalized that they bring to higher education certain similar nontraditional characteristics. Minority students possess a world view, a frame of reference, and culture-specific learning needs different from those of traditional students. Minority students:

- come from diverse cultural backgrounds
- experienced systematic oppression as a minority group member
- have closer family and community ties
- face pressures as first family members to attend college (Wright 1984).

Minority students may be handicapped by poor high school preparation, greater financial needs, higher adjustment needs, and higher levels of expressed academic anxiety (Vasquez and Chavez 1980). As a result, attrition rates for minority students are higher than those for traditional students. Most development theories guiding student affairs are based upon Western notions of human behavior and so may not be appropriate for minority students until they encompass broader cultural, historical, and religious traditions (Wright 1984).

International students

Foreign students are an increasingly significant segment of enrollments in higher education. In 1960, approximately 50,000 foreign students attended colleges or universities; that number increased to 250,000 in 1976–77 (Carnegie Council 1980). It is projected that foreign enrollments will soon top 350,000 ("Foreign Students" 1984). International students are in a special legal situation and must learn to adapt to a different social, cultural, and administrative situation. Practical needs stemming from living in a foreign country must be addressed, in addition to other needs. Difficulty in academic adjustment, particularly centered on problems with English but also dealing with American educational traditions, characterizes international students. Because of cultural differences, tension often arises between international and American students.

Student affairs workers are often unaware of the cultural stress that international students suffer and miss opportunities to respond to those needs. A study of international students at North Carolina State University found that the top five adjustment problems of those students included homesickness, obtaining housing, social relations with the opposite sex, difficulties with the English language, and financial problems (Stafford, Marion, and Salter 1980). Recognition of these needs suggests directions for student affairs professionals.

Part-time students

With the expansion of flexible curricula and scheduling, wider use of instructional media, and increasing numbers of nonresidential institutions, more students are choosing to attend college part time. Many nontraditional groups make up a significant portion of the part-time students attending institutions of higher education. For many of them, because of other commitments and responsibilities, participation in further education would not be possible if full-time residential study were the only option. In addition, students with good job opportunities and the desire to obtain a college degree may increasingly mix work and education in the future (Carnegie Council 1980). With more adult students attending college at all levels on a part-time basis, discrete periods of education and work may become more blended in the future as lifelong learning becomes more desirable, necessary, and attractive to students (Cross 1981a).

Flexibility in the design of academic programs and the delivery of student services characterizes the needs of part-time students. Elements of this flexibility include the variable scheduling of classes, independent study, flexible financial aid, and provision of support services during evening and weekend hours. Furthermore, support services needed by part-time students differ from those of full-time students. Efforts that address the stress of family and job pressures and seek to integrate the student with others in the campus community are important to part-time students. The integration of the various needs of part-time students with institutional priorities and goals is increasingly important to the management of enrollments at many institutions, creating opportunities for the student affairs professional.

Academically underprepared students

Poorly prepared students are one of the largest, fastest growing subgroups in higher education (Astin 1984a), evidenced by the decline in recent years in SAT and ACT scores. But it is not solely nontraditional students who are deficient in basic skills; increasing numbers of traditional students have also been found to need remedial programs (Astin 1984a).

Many students, recently attracted to higher education, have experienced poor preparation in high school, and institutions are responding by developing remedial programs, enhancing academic advising, and establishing learning skills centers for such basic skills as writing and math. These efforts are often part of a larger retention effort (Baldridge, Kemerer, and Green 1982).

Despite sharp declines in academic skills, more students are aspiring to advanced study beyond the bachelor's degree, most prominently in high-level professional fields like medicine, law, dentistry, and business. A disparity between ability and aspiration is often created, and it must be resolved early in the student's college career.

Poorly prepared students need career and educational counseling that seeks to match ability and aspiration in addition to remedial programs addressed to basic skills and study skills. To identify the needs of such students, the University Counseling Service of the University of Iowa conducts needs assessment studies on this special population. The information gathered can help to integrate the special needs of underprepared students with student affairs programs and services and to provide essential student information to other campus programs.

Disabled students

Students with physical or learning disabilities are an increasingly visible and vocal minority group on campuses today. The passage of Section 504 of the 1973 Rehabilitation Act mandating equal opportunity for qualified handicapped people in education programs and activities has stimulated the enrollment of disabled students and required institutions to make necessary accommodations (McBee

Student affairs workers are often unaware of the cultural stress that international students suffer.

1982). In addition, early intervention efforts are resulting in higher educational aspirations for disabled students (Hameister 1984).

Disabled students bring various needs to institutions, including transportation to and around campus, learning assistance that includes interpreters and recorders, removal of architectural barriers in classrooms, residence halls, and other campus facilities, and support services. Preadmission and orientation programs are particularly important for the adjustment of disabled students (Hameister 1984; McBee 1982). Disabled students enrolling in higher education often need support in developing social skills, leadership skills, and a positive self-concept (Hameister 1984). In each of these areas, the student affairs professional may be instrumental in assisting the institution to assimilate this population by overcoming the architectural, institutional, and student services barriers facing these students (Demetrulias, Sattler, and Graham 1982).

Older students
The aspirations, expectations, and needs of older undergraduate students are significantly different from those of 18 to 24 year olds, and that fact, coupled with growing numbers of such students, is affecting the efforts of institutions and student affairs organizations. Already, students over 25 make up over one-third of college students. Many adults seek postsecondary education during a period of transition, and the events that precipitated the transition (divorce, children leaving home, job obsolescence, job competition, and so on) give rise to varying personal, educational, intellectual, and career needs (Greenfeig and Goldberg 1984). The motivations, psychological development, academic readiness, and life/time commitments of older students represent a special collegiate subculture (Kasworm 1980), and the value priorities of adults are significantly different from those of younger students (Pirnot and Dunn 1983).

While adults are choosing to participate in higher education in increasing numbers, technological changes are demanding the reeducation and retraining of significant parts of the population each year. As a result, adults are more actively participating in degree programs and continuing education and are being actively recruited by many institutions (Cross 1981a).

Adults traditionally enter higher education with a high level of motivation and specific educational and vocational goals. But for many, the transition to the college environment can be difficult. Adults exhibit different learning styles, academic and social concerns, and family role obligations (Cross 1981a). A recent study on emerging client populations identified several counseling needs for adult students: adult career development, life span/life cycle role management, reentry in an institution of higher education, and family and market role (Parker and Eliason 1980). In addition, adult students express different practical needs in financial aid, class scheduling, counseling and advising services, and access to learning services.

In response to these varied needs, student affairs professionals are increasingly called upon to accommodate them and to modify their programs and services. Student affairs professionals may be instrumental in integrating the needs of this group with the goals and priorities of the institution. At the University of Maryland, for example, one course emphasizes the important skills and resources needed to help students succeed in college, and it includes assistance in choosing a major and academic advising, career planning and vocational testing, reading and study skills, opportunities to share common experiences, campus resources, and time management.

Summary
The varied needs of nontraditional students have several implications for student services:

- Greater attention to the particular needs of women of all ages as they enter careers and define roles in new ways, which might include the development of women's centers, guidelines to combat harassment, assertiveness training, and day care.
- Attention to the adjustment problems and anxieties of minority students, which might focus on the individual but is also important to institutional efforts aimed at recruitment and retention.
- Attention to the legal, financial, administrative, and adjustment needs of international students, which

might result in international student centers, staff, and programs.

- Flexibility in the delivery of student services to part-time students and the incorporation of issues important to non-campus-based students with multiple commitments in the design of programs.
- The provision of learning assistance to underprepared students, including counseling and advising to help students match expectations and abilities.
- Attention to the physical needs of disabled students, including the development of social and leadership skills and a positive self-concept, which might include an advocate position for disabled students.

Attending to the needs of subpopulations increasingly important to institutions is an important challenge for student affairs, and integrating their needs with the institution's goals and priorities will remain a challenge.

Changing Student Characteristics
In a changing world, even traditional students are not the same as they used to be. Although students of the 1980s resemble their predecessors in many ways—they are concerned about doing well academically, establishing autonomy, seeking supportive interpersonal relationships, and "fitting in" at the institution of their choice—many of their needs, expectations, values, and outlooks are different from those of students of 20 years ago, when many student affairs professionals were trained. Students mirror a changing society through the characteristics they bring to the institution, and among the changing characteristics institutions and student affairs organizations must address are increasing vocationalism, concern for personal success, narcissism, and consumerism, many of which center around growing concerns for success in a chosen career.

Vocationalism
Facing an uncertain future, students are selecting fields they believe will lead to good careers and secure futures. Coupled with a recognition of an evolving information society, this concern is leading to the selection of information-intensive, well-paying professional fields, such as business, law, and engineering (Upcraft, Finney, and Garland 1984).

And while information-intensive professional fields are attracting more students, people-oriented careers and traditional fields in the arts, humanities, and the pure sciences are attracting fewer students (Astin 1984a; Astin and others 1984). According to the Cooperative Institutional Research Project, an ongoing study of the characteristics of entering students, the greatest increase in popularity of fields since 1966 has been in business, computer science, engineering, agriculture, and forestry, with large increases notable in the number of women (Astin and others 1984). On the other hand, participation in the humanities, the fine and performing arts, and the social sciences has declined sharply, accounting for about one-third of all freshmen in 1966 but only one-ninth in 1982.

Career plans parallel these major interests. The increasingly popular fields typically do not require education beyond the bachelor's degree and are relatively high paying (Astin and others 1984). Conversely, those careers requiring advanced training and/or that are relatively low paying (such as the human and social service professions) have demonstrated decreasing popularity. Student vocationalism suggests that students may be interested only in those activities that support or enhance their vocational interests (Levine 1980). As a result, student affairs professionals will have to redouble their efforts to develop the whole person.

Personal success

Although today's students recognize that it will be difficult to achieve success in a competitive world, they are optimistic that as individuals they will be able to achieve it (Astin 1984a). What they may choose to sacrifice or postpone in pursuit of career success—a family, quality of life, personal interests—is very much on the minds of today's students, for diminishing expectations may place the American Dream beyond their grasp (Upcraft, Finney, and Garland 1984). Increased competition further magnifies the current wave of vocationalism (Levine 1980).

Concern for success is reflected in changing student values and life goals; the strongest upward trend is reported in the goal of "being very well off financially" (Astin and others 1984). During the past 10 years, endorsement of this goal has increased from 40 percent of respondents to 70 percent. By contrast, "developing a meaningful philosophy of life" has declined from the most popular goal 15 years ago to the eighth most popular in 1982. Similarly, a recent study of student perceptions of the collegiate experience concluded that most college students still pursue personal development as a part of the collegiate experience but choose to ignore those social and political issues they perceive as having little direct bearing on their personal lives (DeCoster and Mable 1981).

The drive for personal success may be leading to an increase in academic dishonesty (Lamont 1979); reports document the increasing cases of plagiarism, cheating on exams, falsifying lab results, and sabotaging fellow students' projects. Increased academic dishonesty, coupled with little remorse, is a manifestation of the growing narcissistic behavior of students (Suchinsky 1982).

Narcissism

The rise in narcissistic behaviors among students presents new and different kinds of problems to student affairs professionals. Coupled with increasing vocationalism and concern for personal success, student narcissism suggests that students will be most interested in those activities in which they see direct personal benefit, which might include career planning and placement, extracurricular activities that complement career goals, and the like. Further, those administrative and counseling efforts aimed at fostering interpersonal relations and appropriate student conduct will be challenged by self-concerned students (Suchinsky 1982).

Student consumerism

Consumerism has been described as

> *a philosophy of governance (concern for student rights versus college rights) . . . that . . . is premised on a buyer-seller relationship between the student and the college; that . . . seeks rights and remedies off campus as well as on campus; and that . . . is concerned with the rights and remedies of individuals as well as those of the majority* (Levine 1980, pp. 78–79).

While the consumer movement is not new to campuses, several trends explain its recent evolution: the educational marketplace that favors the buyer (the student), the rise in the number of student lobbies, the growing numbers of nontraditional students with special needs, the evidence of more self-interested students, the increased costs of higher education, and the abandonment of *in loco parentis* on most campuses (Davis 1980; Levine 1980).

Student consumerism is related to a greater concern for personal success as well as to narcissistic tendencies. It suggests that students are more active in seeking redress, not through the forms of activism that characterized the 1960s but through more traditional means, such as litigation. And student consumerism is supported indirectly by institutions' concern for maintaining enrollments. One observer predicts that student consumerism will peak in 1990, when demographic conditions will be worst for colleges and best for students (Levine 1980).

Just as student consumerism presents new challenges to the administration of institutions, so too will it affect student affairs organizations. Consumers are more likely to assert individual rights and contractual rights, challenge fairness and due process in administrative action, and seek to receive what they are paying for. As a result, student affairs organizations will need to become more consistent in the development and application of policies and practices. And to the extent that consumers demand programs and services, student affairs staff will need to respond.

Summary
Even as institutions attempt to assimilate new subpopulations, the "traditional" student clienteles to which student affairs organizations addressed much of their efforts in the past are changing. The new "traditional" students are exhibiting different goals and values, educational and career expectations, and interests. They exhibit more vocationalism, greater concern for personal success, growing narcissism, and increasing consumerism than previous generations of students. In their academic life, changing characteristics are reflected in choice of majors and careers.

While these changes have important implications for academic programs, they suggest that student affairs organizations should rethink their programs and services to reflect the changing goals and values of the so-called traditional student. Addressing the needs of nontraditional students while ignoring the evolution of traditional students will result in only a partial response to changing students.

In addition to addressing the needs of new traditional students, student affairs organizations must also translate their needs and goals to faculty and administrators so that they might be more fully reflected in institutional goals. This point is particularly important, as the needs, motivations, and expectations of the "traditional" student are much different from what they were 10 or 20 years ago. To the extent that student affairs professionals are able to interpret these changes to faculty and administrators, they will be able to take the leadership in formulating institutional responses to changing student clienteles. Moreover, cooperative efforts between faculty and student affairs to identify evolving student needs and expectations and to develop strategies to address them will result in more effective academic and student affairs programs.

For the student affairs organization, changing student interests and values have several implications:

- Increased efforts in career planning and placement
- Increased counseling related to helping students to establish reasonable life and career expectations
- Focused attention on developing fair and consistent policies and practices in student discipline and student behavior codes and preparation to address the special behavior problems of narcissistic students
- Increased attention to anxiety caused by changing sex roles and to the development of men and women who may be able to work effectively together
- Increased attention to students' changing preferences for extracurricular activities from community service, politics, and self-governance to career-related, self-interest, and health/fitness activities.

CHANGING INSTITUTIONAL STRATEGIES

Much attention in the mid- to late-1970s was focused on the projected results of demographic and financial trends, changing student clienteles, and changing institutional conditions in higher education, including the management of decline (Boulding 1975), the coming depression in higher education (Cheit 1971), and the imminent "reduction, reallocation, and retrenchment" (Mortimer and Tierney (1979). Others attempted to suggest ways to maintain and improve institutional vitality (Carnegie Council 1975; Mingle and Norris 1981), recommending ways in which state, federal, and institutional leaders could improve the lot of higher education, even as they projected institutional closings, widespread termination of programs, and a lamentable loss of institutional vitality. While the reality has not been as dire as the predictions, institutions have become more cautious and careful in their outlooks. And the lessons learned in the transition from expansion to maintenance and enhancement have not been forgotten.

The past decade was not the only period in which institutions faced uncertain futures. Over the years, higher education has found strategies to preserve or resume growth when faced with conditions that would limit that prospect (Leslie and Miller 1974). Institutions have sought innovative ways to improve productivity, much like business and industry, attempting to revitalize themselves through the following strategies:

1. *The introduction of a new good or grade of good already in use.* The amount of time and the types of degrees have changed to meet new market forces over the years. Examples in the past have been the awarding of baccalaureate degrees for teachers, associate degrees, and external degrees. More recently, institutions have structured programs for part-time students, continuing professional education, and the awarding of associate and baccalaureate degrees as a credential in a wider range of fields.

2. *The introduction of a new method of production, for example, a new type of labor-saving machinery.* Over the years, classes have gotten larger, more graduate teaching assistants have been used, and the media have been more extensively used in higher education.

Credit for previous experience and weekend programs are more recent examples.

3. *The opening of new markets.* This innovation has probably been the most used in higher education. We have a long history of becoming more egalitarian in the types of programs offered and students attracted. Various new student clienteles have become increasingly important to institutions.

4. *The employment of a new source of supply production factors.* Since their Harvard beginnings, institutions have sought financial resources from a variety of sources, including churches, federal, state, and local governments, and auxiliary enterprises. Most recently, institutions have sought voluntary giving from friends, alumni, corporations, and foundations. Similarly, increased management of funds and internal accountability for the use of funds have been sought to get the most out of resources available.

5. *The reorganization of an industry, several industries, or part of an industry, for example, monopolization of some industry.* Higher education institutions have sought to form consortia, joint research institutes, and collaborative efforts with business and industry and with other organizations (Leslie and Miller 1974, pp. 24–25).

To the extent that these efforts have been successful, the bleaker doomsday projections have not been realized; the present condition of higher education in general is better than many in the early 1970s would have predicted. Institutions have adapted by responding to changing conditions—much as they have in the past—but the widespread closings and general erosion have not occurred as predicted. Institutions have changed or redirected their efforts in many ways:

- comprehensive planning (including reduction and reallocation)
- the development of effective information systems
- increased focus on enrollment management (including marketing efforts, retention, and the attraction of nontraditional students)
- employment of preventive law
- active pursuit of private funds

- promotion of business/college partnerships
- effective management of resources and increased internal accountability.

Comprehensive Planning

Planning in higher education has been described as haphazard and ineffective, but growth in the past has been tolerant of mistakes (Bender 1974); current conditions, however, are less tolerant of ineffective planning (Kramer 1980). As a result, colleges and universities are increasingly concerned with planning more effective use of resources to meet the challenges of the future. Institutions could learn much from poor planning and planning mistakes experienced during growth and, from that understanding, plan more effectively for the steady state (Bender 1974). Strategic planning—''an institutionwide, future-examining, participative process resulting in statements of institutional intention that synergistically match program strengths with opportunities to serve society'' (Cope 1981, p. 8)—is a planning method particularly suited to colleges and universities (Keller 1983). It is much different from other planning in the past that focused on internal analysis rather than on more external, open, systems analysis.

Planning in student affairs has been uneven. A recent survey found little organized planning by most student affairs organizations (Priest, Alphenaar, and Boer 1980), and other observers suggest that student affairs organizations have not responded to changing conditions with comprehensive efforts but with often cosmetic changes in programs and services (Biggs and Skinner 1979). More effective planning is needed in the field if it is to meet current and future conditions.

Long-range planning is the key to effective management in student affairs when responding to the changing environment of higher education and student affairs.

No task in the management of student affairs is less attended to than long-range planning. Yet the hard truth is that if we do not plan our future, someone else will plan it for us. The implication is clear: student affairs leaders must find better ways to identify future needs and prepare to meet those needs (Pillinger and Kraack 1981, p. 8).

Student affairs leaders are apparently devoting more time and effort to planning. At the Community College of Allegheny County (Pennsylvania), the student activities division uses a data-based management system to assess students' needs, evaluate programs, and record students' participation. This system has led to improvements in decision making and in meeting the needs of part-time students, adult students, and others. Information stored in the data base is also used to monitor progress toward long-term objectives in the student activities master plan. Similarly, comprehensive strategies for planning, setting goals, and evaluating programs in student affairs have been developed at Stetson University and at Furman University.

Effective Information Systems

Related to institutional planning, and a precondition to effective and insightful planning, is an effective information system. Information systems are important for internal decision making as well as for providing information to external agencies (Balderston 1978), and management information systems aid in decision making and planning functions for both units and institutions as a whole (Baldridge and Tierney 1979).

The application of information technologies holds great promise for student affairs in two ways. First, through the collection and analysis of student and program data, student affairs professionals are able to learn more about students' needs, characteristics, program use and effectiveness, and so on. Student affairs professionals have access to all kinds of information about students, staff, programs, curricular elements, facilities, equipment, and finances (Racippo and Foxley 1980); put in the right form, such information can be used for creative solutions to problems or to capitalize on opportunities for new efforts, to document the need for the development of a new program or the continuation of existing ones. Perhaps most important, it can assist student affairs organizations in the management of existing resources to most effectively meet the needs of students and programs.

Second, information systems assist labor-intensive work, such as the student affairs function. Automated office systems in admissions, financial aid, room assignments, and placement offices, to name a few, are reducing the amount of time spent by professional and support staff on routine activities. Further, computer-assisted guidance systems can help student affairs professionals reach more students with limited staff resources (Sampson 1982).

Student affairs professionals can match a student's needs with programs and services through the increased use of computers, and the goals of recruitment, retention, and referral can be better achieved through the employment of computer technologies. Such surveys as the Student Descriptive Questionnaire or the Student Development Task Inventory can be used to assess the environment and to evaluate students' needs to better develop student affairs (Erwin and Miller 1985).

Data-based management information systems can be used to assist in advising and retaining students. For instance, Miami-Dade Community College uses a computer monitoring system to track students' grades, to warn students of potential problems, to provide feedback on students' performance, and to match career goals and abilities. It has meant more personalized help for students from faculty members who, as a result, possess accurate and up-to-date information for advising students.

. . . A precondition to effective and insightful planning is an effective information system.

Enrollment Management

Enrollment management includes "a host of functions that cross divisional lines, including clarification of institutional purpose, program development, marketing and recruitment, financial aid, orientation, and retention" (Baldridge, Kemerer, and Green 1982, p. 27). In many ways it is similar to and part of a larger institutional planning effort; the two are often complementary. As a set of strategies, enrollment management implies an assertive and informed approach to ensure the number and quality of new students needed by the institution.

> As a process, enrollment management helps institutions:
> (1) develop a keener awareness of their purpose and
> character in relation to the student marketplace; (2)
> improve ties to prospective client groups; and (3) attract
> students into and through the institution (Baldridge,
> Kemerer, and Green 1982, p. 27).

Sixty percent of presidents responding to a survey on enrollment problems agreed that enrollment was a major concern for their institution, and 75 percent reported increased competition for students. Only 16 percent anticipated declining enrollment in the future, however. Thus, despite concern over enrollments, few institutions have developed or implemented comprehensive new student marketing plans or systematic programs for reducing student attrition. Institutions that are serious about retention, however, should take certain steps: (1) develop an "early warning system" to signal advisors and counselors when a student is showing signs of dropping out; (2) develop a strong residence life program and other activities that promote social integration; (3) strengthen academic programs and carefully integrate the academic program with students' needs; (4) focus advising; (5) focus efforts on commuter students; and (6) link recruitment and retention (Baldridge, Kemerer, and Green 1982).

A similar study found recruitment and retention of students to be critical issues for the future (Kinnick and Bolheimer 1984). Marketing and recruiting by higher education are not new in most institutions, and recently, institutions have become increasingly concerned about their attractiveness to a wide range of clienteles and supporters.

Most institutions, however, engage in marketing in a disjointed and haphazard way, falling short of a comprehensive effort (Litten 1980). Interest is increasing, however, in more formal and comprehensive marketing plans as institutions attempt to respond to a number of changing conditions. The "how to" manuals and books, survey research firms offering services to admissions offices to help them better define and reach their markets, and workshops, conferences, and consultant services attest to the growing interest in marketing higher education (Litten 1980).

A comprehensive marketing approach should be formulated for most effective results (Grabowski 1981). In addition, the marketing plan should be developed with the input and support of the entire campus community, not just the offices and functions most directly affected. Before the development of a plan, the market position should be determined, based upon several factors: the institutional mission statement, the institutional image as perceived by its various clienteles and supporters, the types of students attending the institution, and academic programs. After assessing the current market position, the institution might look at the possibility of broadening its market based on a careful assessment of its current position and the potential for an enhanced position. Finally,

Any marketing effort must be student-oriented, assessing and serving the needs and interests of students. However, no institution of higher education should rely solely upon student desires; instead, a school must consider student preferences in the context of its mission and goals . . . to preserve the integrity of its programs (Grabowski 1981, p. 1).

As the division within the institution most responsible for the quality of student life, student affairs is essential in developing a strong marketing posture for the institution. In attempting to market itself, an institution must meet students' needs and, where appropriate, students' desires to present the best possible and most attractive picture. Integrating students' needs with institutional goals is essential in the market posture of any institution. As integrators, student affairs professionals are in a position to address students' needs while supporting the institution's marketing goals and, using its special understanding of students, to modify institutional practices to meet the needs of its prospective clients. The chief student affairs officer has an important role in this effort (Kinnick and Bolheimer 1984; Shay 1984).

Recruitment

Recruitment of students is one element of the enrollment management process that calls for the involvement of student affairs in many ways. With decreasing numbers of traditional students and increasing competition for all students, recruitment on most campuses has increased in recent years. The preparation of new promotional materials to be sent to likely students is the most popular new strategy (Baldridge, Kemerer, and Green 1982). Nevertheless, traditional recruiting methods, such as high school visitations, direct mail, and attendance at college nights and fairs, are the strategies institutions use most frequently (College Entrance Examination Board 1980).

The implications of increased recruitment for student affairs are numerous. Generally, student affairs seeks to develop and enhance student life and promote social integration, both important "selling points" for many institutions. While admissions and financial aid professionals remain central recruitment staff at institutions actively seeking to recruit students, however, many institutions are employing faculty members, alumni, and other administrators in recruitment efforts (Baldridge, Kemerer, and Green 1982). A recent study of college presidents found that the role of chief student affairs officer is critical to recruitment (Kinnick and Bolheimer 1984). In addition to general efforts to support recruitment, student affairs staff are creating weekend and outreach programs that involve faculty, students, and administrators and are designed to recruit highly attractive students to the campus.

Retention
Related to marketing strategies and increased attention to recruitment are efforts to improve the retention of matriculated students. As an enrollment strategy, retention has received considerable attention in recent years. A high attrition rate experienced by an institution may be its single greatest enrollment problem (Stadtman 1980).

The costs of attrition to an institution are numerous, and they multiply over time. Most directly, dropouts or transfers cause a direct loss of tuitions, fees, and auxiliary revenues. Second, a high rate of attrition may affect recruitment efforts by increasing the numbers of students who must be recruited each year and by damaging the often carefully nurtured institutional image. Third, high attrition may undermine the diversity, richness, and cohesiveness within the student body.

Institutions are not the only ones who may lose in student attrition; the individual who, under different circumstances, might have completed his or her education also loses, and the loss to the individual is compounded by the loss of potential contributions to society.

Many institutional strategies have been recommended to reduce attrition, including improved academic advising, personal counseling, skill development for underprepared students, curricular developments and options, and career planning (Baldridge, Kemerer, and Green 1982; Beal and Noel 1980; Stadtman 1980).

Only a small number of retention activities have been

employed by a substantial number of institutions, and few strategies have been judged to be effective (see table 1). Many student affairs efforts are important to institutional retention strategies, however. While recent studies (Baldridge, Kemerer, and Green 1982; Beal and Noel 1980; Stadtman 1980) suggest that few of these activities have great impact on retention, a recent project suggests otherwise. In a demonstration project conducted by Baldridge, eight underenrolled institutions enhanced student services on their campuses and experienced reduced attrition; in some cases, those efforts increased retention by as much as 35 percent (Green 1983).

Developing social integration, an area that traditionally has been the responsibility of student affairs, is an essential

TABLE 1
CAMPUS RETENTION STRATEGIES:
RESULTS OF THREE NATIONAL SURVEYS

Activity	Percent of Colleges Attempting the Activity		Percent Reporting Activity Has Great Impact
	Stadtman (1980)	*Beal and Noel (1980)*	*Baldridge, Kemerer, and Green (1982)*
Orientation, counseling, and advising	55	34	18
Career planning	9	6	6
Learning centers/academic support	36	24	29
Exit interviews	9	3	2
Curricular developments	13	2	6
New policies/grading options	11	4	1
Improved facilities	5	–	–
More financial aid	4	–	6
More student/faculty contact	6	–	–
More service to nontraditional students	3	–	8
Improved student activities and services	7	–	–
Early warning systems	–	12	–
Peer programs	–	4	–
Faculty/staff development	–	3	3
Multiple action programs	–	3	–
Cocurricular activities	–	2	–
Dropout studies	–	2	–
Improved dorm life	–	–	10

Source: Baldridge, Kemerer, and Green 1982, p. 39.

element in retention efforts (Astin 1975). It is increasingly becoming the concern of the entire institution because of its effects on retention (Lenning, Sauer, and Beal 1980), which suggests that the role of student affairs in institutional enrollment management is more central than many realize. When enrollments decline, it is often the student affairs budget that is reduced (Deegan 1981), but this trend may be suicidal, given the potential for enrollment crisis in many institutions (Baldridge, Kemerer, and Green 1982). The student life component may determine the very survival of some institutions.

Creating an environment attractive to students is important to retention (Baldridge, Kemerer, and Green 1982). Strong cooperation among student services, faculty, and other administrators focused on enrollment management can have an enormous influence on the institution's educational and financial viability, and a "renewed emphasis on 'student life' is mandatory for a campus that anticipates enrollment shortfalls" (p. 59). Chief student affairs officers should lead the effort to understand why students leave, where they go, and what efforts lead to their retention (Shay 1984).

Student affairs professionals thus have the potential to serve as "team leaders" in the development and implementation of strategies to manage enrollments. Recent examples demonstrate where student affairs staff, often in conjunction with faculty and other administrators, have put programs aimed at retention into place. For example, Project RETAIN at Carson-Newman College (Tennessee) seeks to provide an opportunity for students and counseling center staff to explore the factors surrounding initial decisions to transfer or drop out. In a similar vein, members of the counseling staff of John Jay College of Criminal Justice developed a course for students on academic probation that seeks to remedy deficiencies in reading and study skills, to assess academic ability, and to help students take responsibility for their academic performance. In each of these cases, student affairs efforts are complemented by faculty efforts to improve retention.

Preventive Law
A student affairs organization that is fully integrated with the goals of the institution will find that it must support

other institutional efforts aimed at responding to changing conditions. A growing reliance on legal staffs and growing legalistic relationships inside and outside the institution are evident (Gouldner 1980; Papler 1977). The growth in the size of legal staffs in the past few years serves as a crude index of the amounts of legal assistance required by colleges and universities.

The practice of preventive law as a strategy is an attempt to comply with legal norms to prevent judicial interference. While it may be regarded as a defensive reaction by colleges and universities to the increasing influence of the courts on higher education, preventive law might also be viewed as active administrative practice to prevent undue court influence on internal affairs. As an approach to dealing with external influences, preventive law ranges from engaging counsel to put institutional policies and procedures in proper legal order to forestall litigation, to judging the impact and interpretation of laws in advance to assist in lobbying.

While students' increased assertiveness in their civil and contractual rights requires the institution in general to respond with an increased understanding of the legal ramifications of its actions, it places particular pressure on the student affairs organization to respond. These responses include a codification of rules, procedures, and policies that ensure due process in disciplinary actions; formalized agreements for housing, food service, and other student services; and formalized procedures and policies for the delivery of student services in all areas. In addition, concern is evident over the institution's liability in its relationship with student groups. In each of these areas, student affairs professionals have felt pressures to modify and formalize processes and to consider future litigation in their policies and practices.

Increasing Private Support
Revenues from private voluntary sources for education and general purposes for institutions have increased dramatically in the past 10 years as a result of efforts by institutions to maintain or increase funding. Recently, The Council for Financial Aid to Education reported that total voluntary support for higher education for 1983–84 reached a record $5.6 billion (Desruisseaux 1985). It should come as

no surprise that private support for institutions, public and private, has become increasingly important. In 1976, gifts and endowments accounted for 3.2 percent of revenues for public institutions and 14.6 percent of revenues for private institutions, but their importance to institutions goes beyond what these figures might indicate (Carnegie Council 1980). These funds are typically the discretionary funds available to support new efforts (Kramer 1980). Increasingly, all parts of the institution are becoming involved in institutional development activities, particularly at small private institutions. Of particular interest to student affairs organizations are efforts to involve student affairs professionals and student volunteers in annual giving and capital campaign efforts.

Today's students make tomorrow's alumni, and interest is growing in fostering a desire for continuing support after graduation while students are still enrolled. Those activities include the creation of student alumni corps, the involvement of senior students in class fund raising, and the involvement of students in alumni activities. In each of these efforts, student affairs organizations often provide direct and indirect support; in many institutions, the chief student affairs officer is integrally involved in fund raising and alumni support. The chief student affairs officer may in fact be instrumental in identifying and organizing students to cultivate and solicit support among alumni (Shay 1984).

Student affairs organizations may also be involved in parents associations, with the dual purpose of enhancing the parent/student/campus relationship and encouraging annual support from interested and able parents. Research conducted on students at Pennsylvania State University demonstrated the importance of the parent/student relationship in both the academic and social/emotional development of students during the college years (Upcraft, Peterson, and Moore 1981). As a result, the student affairs organization there was instrumental in establishing a parents association to keep parents better informed and to involve them where appropriate in the development of students. In conjunction with the university development office, parallel efforts are made to increase private giving on behalf of the organization.

Likewise, many student affairs organizations are working with and managing private funds that have been made available to support student services. These funds might include named and general scholarship funds, funds to support cultural activities managed by student activities offices, and endowment funds used to support the improvement and renovation of residence halls.

Thus, the involvement of student affairs staff in the attraction of gifts and the management of endowment funds is growing. Efforts to increase these funds is an institutional response in which student affairs staffs are increasingly engaged.

Changing Relationship of Business and Colleges

For the past 100 years or so, colleges and universities have nurtured informal relationships with business and industry and vice versa. These relationships have recently become more frequent and more formal. They too have important implications for student affairs.

As business has become more complex, so too has its relationship with colleges and universities. In this century, a college education has become a necessary credential with which to pursue many careers in business and industry. Beginning with the research demands created by a nation at war, research universities and the industrial community increasingly joined to expand technological frontiers. Recently, business and industry and educational institutions have seen that collaboration is becoming increasingly important to the future vitality of both.

Events of the last decade have shaken the confidence of the educational and industrial communities, both of which are recognizing that isolation from the other has contributed to their present predicament. In turn, each perceives increased collaboration as a way of improving the health of higher education and the competitive position of American business. . . . Higher education and industry are, as a consequence, becoming increasingly aware of their underlying interdependence (Matthews and Norgaard 1984, pp. 1–2).

Examples of cooperative efforts include research activities, grants of equipment, sharing of facilities and personnel, and general and programmatic support. As a result, many units within the institution are increasingly involved in supporting partnerships. For student affairs, business and college partnerships provide increased opportunities for student internships and practicums, summer placement, cooperative education programs, networks for career exploration and placement, and the involvement of business men and women in helping students bridge the worlds of academe and business. In addition to involvement in programs, business and industry can provide direct support for career planning and placement; for instance, funds solicited from businesses typically recruiting students at Penn State were used to construct a new interviewing center. Finally, mutually supportive relations between colleges and businesses provide additional opportunities for corporate scholarships and training programs, important to the attraction of career-conscious students.

Management of Resources
Declining enrollment and funding, in addition to increased accountability to state and federal agencies and courts, argue for more effective management in higher education. As a result of these trends, management theories, practices, and strategies have been increasingly applied in and recommended for higher education. The number of books focusing on management strategies in higher education and the number of management institutes for educational leaders and consulting firms have increased in recent years.

Several handbooks attest to the growing interest in management applications in student affairs; they include a manual on planning, budgeting, and evaluation for student affairs organizations (Harpel 1976), a volume dedicated to the application of management techniques in student affairs that covers such topics as management by objective, management information systems, budgeting, and performance appraisal systems (Foxley 1980a), and a handbook on student services that offers chapters on management tools for student affairs staff (Delworth, Hanson, and associates 1980). A new, more central role for student affairs is calling for greater expertise in management, and although student affairs professionals have only slowly responded to demands for more effective management (Meabon et al. 1981), some evidence indicates that the application of management strategies is growing in many institutions.

Internal Accountability

As a result of constant or decreasing dollars, demands for new programs and services while maintaining existing programs, and increased accountability to state, federal, and accrediting agencies, internal accountability is growing. Departmental and divisional budgets as well as programs and activities in many institutions are scrutinized carefully; budgets are increasingly lean and requests for additional funding must be accompanied by careful and reasoned justifications.

A study of accountability demands on student affairs programs undertaken by the NASPA Division of Research and Program Development found that institutions face more demands for program information from state agencies and governing boards (Harpel 1975). These demands most frequently include requests for data on program outcomes and impact and for documentation of needs for certain services. Unfortunately, as a consequence of these requests, 20.2 percent of all institutions report a reduction in student affairs staff and 32.6 percent report reductions in overall funding or funding for specific services.

Even though funding for student affairs has not lost as much ground as feared, interest in accountability remains (Barnes, Morton, and Austin 1984), although the design and implementation of accountability systems for student affairs appears to be minimal. A model of accountability for student affairs can thus be based on four general elements: (1) identification of educational goals and performance objectives; (2) development of alternative strategies for achieving goals and performance objectives; (3) periodic evaluation of personnel and program performance; and (4) inclusion of nonpractitioners in educational decision making (Barnes, Morton, and Austin 1984).

Critical to any accountability system is the availability of information concerning programs, costs, and effectiveness. Information in this area is growing, particularly as a result of increasing use of computers. To respond to questions of accountability, student affairs research and evaluation must be increased to provide evidence of effectiveness (Brown 1985a).

Summary

The responses to changing conditions employed by institutions typically have important implications for student affairs organizations. As institutions expanded in the 1950s and 1960s, student and academic affairs often pursued separate but parallel goals in serving increasing numbers of students. Although this approach was tolerated during periods of expansion (in some cases it may have proved beneficial to the institution), current conditions argue for a more coordinated and integrated approach to promote institutional viability and vitality. Responding to changes in students, in society, and in higher education, institutions and student affairs organizations stand ready to work together to improve enrollment management, promote partnerships between business and college, increase private support, engage in preventive law, develop information systems, and attempt more effective planning. The involvement of student affairs in these activities is reshaping its role to one that is more central to and integrated with institutional goals and priorities, a role that moves student affairs beyond the internal management of student life to a partnership with faculty and administrators that is concerned with the whole institution and its responses to changing conditions. In that role, the student affairs professional may be seen increasingly as one who seeks to integrate the goals of individual development with institutional development (Borland 1980). To meet the demands of a new role, however, the student affairs professional must have a sound understanding of the role, the skills it calls for, and the programs and services it demands.

THE INTEGRATOR: A New Role Explained

Since the late 1800s, faculty have transferred much of their responsibility for the social, affective, and moral development of students to student personnel professionals, while retaining responsibility for the cognitive development of students. Likewise, the central mission of institutions—once both moral and academic—has become more purely academic, and as a result attention to the moral and affective development of students has been reduced to a supportive role. In this century, growing numbers of student affairs staff have assumed responsibility for the student's out-of-class experiences, even as the student affairs function settled into its support role.

As the profession grew, it sought to define itself as a special profession within the higher education community. Engaging in this pursuit, however, may have unwittingly encouraged the belief that the student affairs function is significantly less critical than that performed by faculty. By establishing the affective domain as its province—that is, a domain supportive of cognitive development—student affairs positioned itself away from the intellectual heart of the institution. In 1970, McConnell questioned whether student affairs was peripheral or central to the institution. Concluding that it was peripheral, he offered strategies for becoming more central. Today, the same question is raised, and some indications exist that, at least when it comes to budgetary decisions, student affairs is often considered more expendable than other functions believed to be more critical (Deegan 1981; Nelson and Murphy 1980).

Recognition is growing, however, that in serving students, student affairs leaders are serving the institution in ways that are increasingly important to institutional vitality and viability. That is, efforts to integrate diverse student groups, serve students' needs and interests, and improve the management of the institution are resulting in important benefits for institutions—the ability to attract and retain students, to foster supportive alumni, and to manage itself more effectively. Furthermore, those student affairs efforts designed to involve students—on-campus employment, enhanced residential experiences, and appropriate student activities—enhance the educational experience of students and contribute to the quality of education. Indeed, involvement in education has become a matter of national concern

By establishing the affective domain as its province . . . student affairs positioned itself away from the intellectual heart of the institution.

and attention that recognizes the significance of student affairs (Study Group 1984).

Participation in coordinated efforts aimed at responding to changing conditions suggests an integrating role for student affairs. Student affairs is able to take the lead in formulating and implementing responses by integrating students' needs and traditional student affairs goals on one hand and institutional goals and priorities on the other (Shaffer 1973; Silverman 1971, 1980). Assuming leadership for institutional responses that result in benefits to both students and institutions—to realize the potential of the role of integrator—is a natural evolution of the student affairs role that offers the potential to place student affairs in a pivotal role within the institution.

While institutional leaders may be more able to see the direct contribution of student affairs in achieving institutional goals, the contribution of student affairs to faculty efforts may be more difficult to see. For it to occur, student affairs professionals will need to gain greater credibility and respectability within the institution by becoming more involved and visible throughout the institution. For instance, involvement and leadership in enrollment management, retention, advising and counseling nontraditional students, and academic support will increase opportunities for interaction between faculty and student affairs staffs. Likewise, efforts to articulate and address needs of nontraditional and changing traditional students offer opportunities for student affairs staff to be seen in an expert professional role.

Integration may also occur through the attempts of student affairs to become more "facultylike" by teaching, conducting research, and presenting findings—inside and outside the institution—so that the profession gains credibility and respectability within the academic community. Similarly, the involvement of faculty in student affairs— cocurricular activities such as academic interest houses and orientation—offers increased opportunities for interaction, understanding, and appreciation.

Before discussing the elements of this new role of student affairs staff as integrators within the institution, two opposing motivations within the profession must be reviewed—the first because it mitigates against this new role and must therefore be modified in light of it and the second because it supports that new role.

Two Opposing Motivations

Two opposing motivations have characterized the student affairs profession during most of this century. On the one hand, the field of student affairs has attempted to establish itself as a profession distinct from the academic profession (Mueller 1961) through the adoption of theories to guide practice, by the development of a philosophy to guide its efforts, by the establishment of a body of literature for the field, and by the specialized preparation of professionals. As higher education has grown more complex, the student affairs specialist has further specialized into discrete functional roles. In pursuit of professional status, however, student affairs has focused on its own issues while neglecting issues of importance to the institution and the relationship of student affairs to the remainder of the institution. Convinced of its own importance, the student affairs organization can be faulted for not translating that importance to other campus constituencies—faculty, students, and administrators—and in so doing has become alienated from the academic heart of the institution (McConnell 1970). The importance of student affairs has rarely been convincingly argued outside of the profession, which does not diminish its role but rather reminds us that outside constituencies do not necessarily accept the contribution of student affairs on faith.

On the other hand, one of the major goals of student affairs has been to foster the integration of academic and student life. The expansion of student affairs in the late nineteenth and early twentieth centuries was, in large part, the result of attempts to bridge the curriculum and the extracurriculum, providing adult advice and support for those activities neglected by faculty and demanded by students. But what started out as a bridge has evolved into a separate structure and profession within the institution.

The perpetuation of separate administrative structures and goals for academic and student affairs has obvious limitations for effective and imaginative use of talent and resources (Rickard 1972). Student affairs and academic units have often pursued different goals, but changing conditions are calling for coordinated institutional responses involving faculty, administrators, and student affairs professionals (Baldridge, Kemerer, and Green 1982). The efforts made by student affairs, in a time of limited financial and personnel resources, must parallel and support similar institutional efforts (Kinnick and Bolheimer 1984; Shay 1984). Hence, the student affairs professional must integrate the traditional student affairs role with a new, more central role within the institution.

Moving Student Affairs into the Mainstream

Times are no longer prosperous for higher education. Institutions are facing declining enrollments, financial uncertainty, and greater accountability. Students are changing, and increasing numbers of nontraditional students are enrolling. The reality of changing financial conditions and student clienteles leads many institutions to seek areas for budget cuts, which in some institutions leads to questions about the role of student affairs and its importance to the institution. Evidence suggests that student affairs has been cut back as much or more as other departments in many institutions, and in some cases it has been eliminated or radically altered (Deegan 1981; Nelson and Murphy 1980). Because of the functional and philosophical separation of student affairs from the central goals and priorities of many institutions, its inability to justify programs in terms that institutional managers are able to understand, and an inability to articulate the goals of student affairs in terms meaningful to others in the institution, student affairs is questioned on many campuses (Deegan 1981). These threats, however, should not dictate an unchallenged retreat: Institutional responses to changing conditions provide opportunities for the involvement and leadership of student affairs.

Institutions can use four techniques to resist decline: retention, improving student life and the campus climate, tightening standards to attract bright students, and attracting new sources of revenue (Mingle and Norris 1981). Clearly, student affairs is central to the accomplishment of the first two and supportive of the last two. Responses to changing conditions offer opportunities for student affairs to maintain its professional goals while building stronger bridges within the institutional community, which can be accomplished most notably through cooperative efforts aimed at resisting decline. It will call for a redirection of student affairs and its role, however. Threats to student affairs are very real today, but so too are the opportunities.

The student services sector has been primarily a reactive group. I suggest that it must become proactive if it is to survive the next ten years as an effective and integral part of the higher education community. It must learn to anticipate and control its environment. If it doesn't, I suggest, it will become extinct. Not in the sense that it will disappear totally, but in the sense that the form and substance of student services will be so altered that they will be hardly recognizable as having any relationship to those . . . we have known in the past. For just as other elements within higher education and society at large have disappeared . . . so will student services disappear as a functional element within higher education if we do not carefully plan and anticipate our future course (Brodzinski 1978, p. 3).

Others have warned that, while student affairs has been handling the day-to-day needs of students and institutions, it has failed to plan adequately for the future (Priest, Alphenaar, and Boer 1980).

Student affairs divisions have many chances to capitalize on the opportunities suggested by changing conditions. It is a matter of proactively changing to meet conditions.

[By] anticipating the changes, trends, and developments [that] will affect higher education and the student population, we can reconceptualize our approach to student services. . . . We must recognize that the need for many of the services that we traditionally provided has been irrevocably changed or nullified by circumstances totally beyond our control and that our techniques for providing such services have, in many instances, been rendered obsolete by technological and managerial developments (Brodzinski 1978, p. 5).

Never before has the student affairs profession stood on the threshold of such great opportunity (Hurst 1980). But to capitalize on opportunities presented in responding to changing conditions, student affairs professionals must assess their contributions to the institution and its students, now and in the future; work cooperatively with others in the institution to integrate those activities more completely with the mission of the institution and its responses to changing conditions; and become, even more than is the case now, experts on students and their needs and more active in communicating that knowledge to the rest of the college community.

In doing so, student affairs leaders create opportunities to move from the periphery of the institution to its center, allowing student affairs to weather the storm of current conditions and to emerge with an enhanced role in the institution. During financial austerity, "by initiating bold, informed, and creative policies and practices, it may be possible to increase the institutional influence of student affairs" (Kuh 1981, p. 36). And "an alert, assertive response to these forces [changing conditions] will make student affairs essential to institutional effectiveness and therefore worthy of adequate support" (Shaffer 1984, p. 112).

The potential of student affairs has been equated to that of integrators within industrial firms (Silverman 1980). By sharing orientations with students, faculty, and administrators—but bordering on all of these subsystems—the student affairs professional stands in a position to integrate the orientations and goals of the various subsystems. Thus, integrators in student affairs are facilitators who work for the achievement of the goals of the institution and its many subsystems while still retaining professional and student loyalties. They integrate their traditional roles of educator, advisor, and advocate with an institutional outlook promoting organizational development (Borland 1980).

New opportunities for leadership by student affairs indicate that student affairs efforts are evolving from efforts meaningful to the goals of student affairs to efforts meaningful to high-priority, institutional goals; becoming more integrated with faculty efforts; and integrating consumer orientation with theoretical orientations. These trends are occurring as student affairs professionals respond to changing conditions in society, in their institutions, and in the students they serve.

Integration of Goals
The mission of student affairs has always, in the broadest sense, reflected that of the institution and vice versa. The

particular goals, objectives, and efforts of the institution and student affairs have not always been coordinated, however. This situation is not necessarily unproductive for the institution, but with financial uncertainty and the need to respond to changing conditions, pressure increases for the responses of the institution and those of its student affairs staff to be integrated. Institutions are seeking to meet the various needs of students and those of new student clienteles in activities like academic advising and personal counseling, career planning, study skills, and learning assistance. These activities increasingly include the efforts of many within the institution, but especially the student affairs staff. Similarly, student affairs staff are encouraging students to become involved in alumni and development efforts while enrolled, in anticipation of increased support later. It is, however, in the area of attraction and retention of students that the integration of student affairs and the institution is presently most apparent.

Recruitment and marketing

Several recent sources have discussed the potential contribution of student affairs to the attraction and retention of students. With the increasing competition for students, the role of student affairs in creating a supportive, developmental, and challenging campus life will be important to the attraction and retention of potential students (Brodzinski 1978). The quality of student life will become increasingly important in marketing aimed at traditional as well as nontraditional students. "The future belongs to those colleges that make the quality of student life their primary mission" (Lewis, Leach, and Lutz 1983), and the ability of the institution and its student affairs organization to demonstrate programs, services, and methods of delivery attractive to students, especially nontraditional students, will be increasingly important.

Evidence suggests strongly that images and perceptions about an institution influence an individual's decision to enroll in a particular college, and the decision to attend a particular college is prompted by a decision to spend four years in a pleasant and rewarding environment and to seek an education that will lead to career and social success (Grabowski 1981). The extent to which the efforts of student affairs contributes to that environment and supports those educational goals will determine the importance of student affairs to institutional marketing. Everyone, from the president down to the students, should be involved in institutional marketing (Grabowski 1981); therefore, all student services staff will need to develop increased expertise in recruitment and retention (Davis 1980).

Involvement in recruiting provides a special opportunity for student affairs to gain visibility, demonstrate its abilities, and use its understanding of students to become more centrally involved in the direction of the institution. Student affairs is in a position to conduct and disseminate research on students' needs and wants and the extent to which the institution provides for them. Engaging in retention studies, student affairs professionals are able to provide information on what attracts and retains students and increase its importance to institutional decision makers (Shay 1984).

Retention
Related to the marketing of the institution and the attraction of students is the retention of matriculated students. Among other features that distinguish the persister from the nonpersister are the following:

- high levels of involvement with the college
- receipt of scholarships, grants, and/or part-time employment on campus
- living in college residence halls
- high quality and use of student support services, especially opportunities for learning assistance, advising, and both academic and nonacademic involvement (Lenning, Sauer, and Beal 1980, pp. 2–3).

In addition, several strategies have been identified as effective in improving student retention:

1. *Admissions and recruiting. When students receive adequate and accurate information from a college, they will be more likely to choose the institution that best meets their needs, which, in turn, will increase their chances of persisting.*
2. *Advising. Improved academic advising . . . in most cases is found to contribute to retention.*
3. *Counseling. Counseling has served as a foundation for numerous retention programs with positive results.*

4. **Early warning and prediction.** *Prediction of potential dropouts can be productive and when combined with one or several early warning strategies can reduce attrition.*

5. **Exit interviews.** *Even though their observed impact on retention is lower than most other intervention strategies, exit interviews can gather significant information on why students leave and how the institution might change to improve the retention for other students. In addition, a few individuals may remain in the institution as a result of assistance gained through an exit interview.*

6. **Extracurricular activities.** *The literature indicates that more often than not meaningful participation in extracurricular activities contributes to student retention.*

7. **Faculty, staff, and curricular development.** *The frequency and quality of faculty and student interactions can contribute positively to student retention, and inservice faculty/staff development efforts can contribute more favorable student/faculty interaction. Changes in curricular design and emphasis also can be productive.*

8. **Financial aid.** *Assisting students to cope with their financial problems can contribute to retention, as can specific types of aid given to students, including scholarships, grants, and on-campus part-time employment.*

9. **Housing.** *Many studies have demonstrated that on-campus housing, including residence halls [and fraternity and sorority houses], improve students' chances of retention.*

10. **Learning and academic support.** *Learning and academic support services . . . clearly . . . have a positive effect on student retention.*

11. **Orientation.** *Institutions that focus on orientation as a retention strategy [show significantly improved retention rates].*

12. **Policy change.** *Colleges that redesign policies and procedures for the purpose of improving student retention show significant improvement in their retention rates* (Lenning, Sauer, and Beal 1980, pp. 3–4).

As can be surmised from this list, most of the retention strategies outlined call for extensive involvement, if not leadership, by student affairs professionals. Moreover, by participating in these retention efforts, student affairs stands to gain from increased partnerships between student affairs staff and faculty.

Integration of Faculty and Student Affairs Efforts
The integration of student development concepts and the academic community has been a goal of most student development educators. Indeed, the integration of academic and student affairs goals is a precondition to the success of student development (Benezet 1979; Brown 1972; Miller and Prince 1977; Smith 1982). Now more than ever, conditions argue for a greater integration of academic and student life. Concern for academic quality, attention to the needs of diverse student groups, and efforts to manage enrollments all argue for coordinated responses. Furthermore, growing concern for the quality of the academic experience argues for coordinated responses. The coordination of all campus professionals to address these concerns and conditions provides significant motivation for greater campus integration.

New efforts in response to changing conditions may blur the traditional roles of faculty, student affairs, and administration. Working together to meet changing conditions will increase the opportunities for greater understanding and integration between faculty and student affairs staff. Several opportunities for joint efforts exist: (1) the recruitment of and provision of programs for high-ability students; (2) academic and career advising; (3) attention to the cognitive and affective needs of new student clienteles; and (4) institutionwide enrollment management. Furthermore, expanded roles for student affairs professionals that increase their credibility and respectability in the institution (teaching, research, and evaluation, for example) will make student affairs professionals more equal partners in the educational enterprise.

Several strategies have been suggested for integrating student personnel work with academic programs (Jones 1978, p. 6). First, student personnel professionals can participate in activities by which students plan their academic programs and monitor their progress toward academic goals. This strategy would mean involvement by student personnel administrators as well as faculty in admissions, orientation, program planning, and program review. Second, student affairs professionals and faculty can collaborate in the areas of teaching, curriculum, and non-class-related field experiences, which might include the involvement of student affairs staff in learning assistance and faculty involvement in cocurricular interest houses. Third, short-term structured educational experiences planned and implemented jointly by faculty and student affairs can involve both groups in the student's total educational process. Academic credibility should be an important goal of professional development for student affairs professionals (Cox and Ivy 1984).

Various strategies employed at the University of Maine at Farmington, for example, integrate the efforts of faculty and student affairs staff—using consulting faculty as experts, recognizing faculty efforts, welcoming new faculty and explaining the role of student affairs, keeping faculty informed of student affairs efforts through newsletters, and engaging in one-on-one liaisons. At the university, not one single effort but a combination of efforts leads to a more positive, mutually supportive relationship (Geller 1982).

Collaboration in the area of student research is another area that holds promise for the integration of efforts (Benezet 1979). Faculty, in conjunction with student affairs workers, could assemble the requisite expertise and personnel power to learn information beyond what is currently known about students. Involving institutional researchers in student research can further enhance the collaboration of faculty and student affairs staff. Studies of factors leading to retention or student achievement can offer one area for joint research. A greater research effort is necessary if the status of the profession is to approach that of the academic profession (Hurst 1980).

Evolving Consumer Orientation
Student affairs professionals have always been concerned with the needs of student clienteles. The programs and services that arise to address those needs, however, may evolve from the expressed desires of students or from theoretical or conceptual notions of the needs of students and the interests and expertise of staff. In most cases, student

affairs organizations provide efforts based on both. Recent attention in the literature to student development theories might suggest a more widespread acceptance of the student development concept as the basis for the development of student affairs programs and services than is perhaps the case. Knowledge of student development theory within the profession and the applications of practice to theory is not widespread, however (Kuh et al. 1977). Instead, many student affairs staff use informal "theories in action" to guide their work with students (Kuh 1981). Student affairs thus is a profession in search of a philosophy (Stamatakos and Rogers 1984).

While the profession continues to develop and assert its conceptual base, changing conditions may argue for a stronger consumer orientation or attention to expressed and directly observable student needs, which may or may not parallel theoretically derived needs. It will be the challenge of the student affairs integrator to address those needs within the context of institutional goals and priorities.

Beyond "theories in action," student personnel professionals are guided in their attempts to assist and develop students with institutional demands for the provision of certain services and with students' demands for services. Responding to the needs of the institution in addition to those of the various student populations, the student affairs staff may be able to enhance their position within the institution. In institutions where the attraction and retention of students is critical to survival and vitality of the institution, the desires of the consumer become more important. Providing those services deemed important by the institution and the student may work to enhance the position of student affairs.

The theoretical base of the profession can be described as inconsistent. Entering student personnel professionals, usually exposed to student development concepts, do not possess a sound theoretical grounding in student development theory or other related theories (Strange and Contomanolis 1983). Moreover, those theories have been challenged, even in their nascent state, as being inappropriate to most nontraditional students (Wright 1984). Work continues in the application of human development theory to the college and university setting, but practitioners still rely on experience or expressed student demands to guide their efforts. It is not unreasonable to say that, while student affairs moved toward establishing a theoretical basis for the profession in the 1960s and 1970s, recent challenges to those theories and changing conditions suggest that its theoretical base will coexist with a consumer orientation.

That conclusion is drawn on the basis of several notions. First, no established theory or philosophy generally guides the profession at this point. Strides have been made in the past 20 years (including the Tomorrow's Higher Education Project and recent work by Knefelkamp (1978) and Stamatakos and Rogers (1984), among others), but without a well-developed, generally understood theory to guide the profession, other factors, such as consumer needs, may be important in guiding efforts.

Second, as dollars become tight, those activities that succeed in fulfilling students' expressed needs and are consonant with institutional goals (such as retention) will be attractive to institutional leaders. Programs designed to meet students' expressed needs will be more justifiable to decision makers than programs designed to meet needs that are not self-reported. And those programs that enhance institutional efforts in recruitment, retention, placement, and eventual alumni support will be more attractive to the institution, regardless of theoretical support. With more astute and demanding educational consumers, student affairs may be in a position where consumer demands must be met. But providing effective responses may, in the long run, enhance the position of student affairs.

Third, different groups are demanding different services and programs. New programs and services for these special clienteles are already expanding on many campuses, including centers for returning adults, women, and minority students and student affairs officers (admissions recruiters, financial aid administrators, and career and personal counselors) employed to deal with the special needs of various nontraditional student groups. Visible, organizational responses to the needs of nontraditional students may be necessary to justify the student affairs effort generally and to increase the attractiveness of the institution to these student groups.

These observations do not preclude or replace well-reasoned, theoretically based efforts in response to changing conditions. In fact, they would arguably be among the strongest efforts. They do, however, imply a primary response to students and institutional consumers of the services and programs of student affairs.

Developing a Greater External Focus
Attention to professional issues and students' needs has never been the solitary focus of the profession, but they have characterized student affairs organizations. A changing world, however, demands attention, and the focus of the new student affairs professional will be broader and more external. The effective student personnel professional must be able to step back from the operational issues and analyze how he or she can help the president and the institution handle external, future-oriented issues (Shay 1984).

As student personnel developed as a profession in the 1960s, its view remained internal, to itself as a profession and to the students it sought to serve. As institutions themselves have become more externally focused, pressures are placed on student affairs to likewise gain a greater external focus. Changing conditions call upon student affairs to become more integrally involved in the goals and priorities of the institution; it must look beyond itself to the institution and to society. To this end, student affairs professionals should continuously assess the institutional environment (Shaffer 1984).

An external focus is exhibiting itself in several ways on campuses and in the profession. First, the understanding of student demographics critical to a more informed participation in recruitment, retention, academic achievement, and placement efforts is emphasized more.

Second, student affairs organizations are involved in efforts to establish bridges to the outside community that bring students into the institution and that place them in appropriate careers and vocations. Involvement in these activities increasingly involves student affairs in the external environment of the institution.

Third, a greater understanding of different student groups and their special needs, educational expectations, and life experiences allows student affairs professionals to share their knowledge of students within and without the institution.

Fourth, involvement with faculty and administration on matters of central concern to the institution provides student personnel administrators with the opportunities and challenges of articulating students' needs and institutional responses. Student affairs professionals who promote student development must also seek to promote organizational development (Borland 1980).

Fifth, providing programs and services for special populations involves student personnel workers in the classroom, the home, the community, and the workplace more than in the past. Similarly, meeting the changing needs of traditional populations moves student affairs workers around the campus and the community.

Sixth, increasing legalism, institutional accountability, and planning and management call for the involvement of student affairs with institutional leaders and faculty. As a result, the implications of these activities are being incorporated into the efforts of student affairs organizations.

Seventh, professional activities like research, evaluation, and teaching bring student affairs staff out of the organization and into faculty settings, and they have the potential to increase the credibility and respectability of the profession.

Summary
Changing conditions argue for a new role for student affairs, one that integrates student, faculty, and institutional goals in the educational enterprise. Bridging the institution's and the students' needs and integrating academic and student affairs will serve to expand and strengthen the role of student affairs within the institution.

> *In short, . . . a number of forces and trends . . . are changing the nature and effectiveness of student affairs. The complex nature of the problems facing society is reflected in the problems of colleges and universities and amply demonstrates the difficulties of the profession. The challenge is not merely to work harder or longer but to perform duties and functions creatively and visibly so that there can be no institutional doubt as to the essential nature of student development oriented programs and services* (Shaffer 1984, p. 114).

To serve an integrating role within the institution calls on student affairs professionals to develop a new outlook, new skills, and new and enhanced programs and services. It further calls on them to engage in continuing professional education to assist in their evolution into this new role and to take a serious and critical look at the adequacy of current models of graduate preparation for the demands of the new role.

IMPLICATIONS FOR PROGRAMS, SERVICES, AND PROFESSIONAL SKILLS

Responses to changing conditions and changing student clienteles and the evolving role as integrator argue for new student affairs efforts and a variety of new skills for student affairs professionals. The challenge of student affairs for the future will be our ability to design and implement new or expanded services and to develop skills suitable to a new role within the institution.

New Skills for Professionals

Just as responses to changing conditions offer the role of student affairs both threats and opportunities, so too does reconceptualizing that role create challenges and opportunities for student affairs professionals. Student affairs professionals as integrators find themselves in different settings demanding new and enhanced skills.

The student affairs professional has been described as an administrator, a counselor/consultant, a student development educator, an environmental designer, and a student advocate (Mendenhall, Miller, and Winston 1982), and these roles are not likely to change in the future. Integrating these roles and the goals they seek to achieve with changing institutional goals, however, is an emerging challenge for student affairs professionals. Meeting this challenge will require new skills.

The acquisition of these skills will to a large extent determine the effectiveness of the student affairs professional in meeting the challenges of a stronger and more central role in institutional responses to changing conditions. His or her ability to integrate human relations skills (the traditional student affairs skills) and organizational skills (the new skills) will to a large extent determine the future of student affairs.

His or her ability to integrate human relations skills and organizational skills will to a large extent determine the future of student affairs.

Among the skills the integrator must possess in a new role are management skills, political skills, research skills, and organizational skills.

Management skills

Among the most important skills that leaders in student affairs need to become integrators are management skills. As a result of efforts to manage institutions more effectively, student affairs administrators are "expected to be familiar with management principles and techniques demonstrating that their offices and programs accomplish what they set out to accomplish'' (Foxley 1980a, p. vii). While the movement to employ management skills in student affairs continues to gain momentum on many campuses, few administrators are trained in management techniques, little emphasis is given to management problems in professional preparation programs, and the literature applying management concepts to student affairs is almost nonexistent (Foxley 1980a). Not all student affairs professionals will necessarily become managers and administrators—one could argue that direct service providers like counselors do not need management skills—the field and those who aspire to management positions will need to possess these skills in greater depth.

Student affairs organizations must employ management techniques to a greater degree if they are to effectively respond to changing conditions (Aery and Moore 1976). But few institutions consistently attempt to employ management tools like the formulation of mission statements, the formulation of goals related to institutional goals, the development of job descriptions, and the implementation of formal evaluations (Meabon et al. 1981).

Management skills should be in addition to, not replacements for, the traditional skills of student affairs professionals; however, more attention must be directed toward them if student affairs is to capitalize on the opportunities that have been presented to it. Management skills may be more important to effective student affairs organizations than knowledge of human development theories (Kuh 1981). The areas in which student affairs leaders must develop improved skills are planning, information processing, financial management, and human resource management.

Planning. Many writers have emphasized the necessity of effective planning for student affairs (see, for example, Biggs and Skinner 1979; Priest, Alphenaar, and Boer 1980; and Saurman and Nash 1975). This attention notwithstanding, very little systematic, organized planning is reported to occur in most student affairs organizations.

In some instances, in fact, it appear[s] that student services may become ends in themselves rather than services designed to support the primary missions of the campus. At such institutions, it may become increasingly difficult to justify, in terms of budgetary support, many of the student services functions (Priest, Alphenaar, and Boer 1980, p. 3).

Student affairs administrators have responded to changing conditions with a variety of hastily made, often cosmetic, changes in programs and services and in administrative structures (Biggs and Skinner 1979). Even though student personnel workers are often consumed with day-to-day issues, with little time left for effective planning, student affairs leaders must be able to accommodate both predicted and unpredicted changes. In short, student affairs planning often suffers from being reactive when it should be proactive (Biggs and Skinner 1979).

Evidence is growing, however, that planning in student affairs is becoming more systematic and comprehensive. At Stetson University (Florida), an integrated planning and evaluation model—POWS (for "problems, objectives, and workshops")—was developed, and Furman University (South Carolina) employs the SWOTS approach (for "strengths, weaknesses, opportunities, and threats) to assess program status and emphasis.

Many of the new planning efforts rely heavily on improved information processing. Acquisition of Data for Accountability and Management (ADAM) at Frostburg State College (Maryland) allows counseling center staff to better plan efforts to meet clients' needs because they have more and more usable information. Similarly, the Student Affairs Program Evaluation Process at the University of Nebraska–Lincoln provides student affairs leaders with better information on which to make decisions for the future.

Planning is critical to student affairs organizations seeking to address changing needs and to take advantage of opportunities to exert leadership in developing institutional responses to changing conditions. Without appropriate planning skills, student affairs may be unable to redirect its efforts to meet changes effectively and to actively determine its future. Various planning models and strategies have been suggested (Biggs and Skinner 1979; Priest, Alphenaar, and Boer 1980; Saurman and Nash 1975), but few have been widely adopted. Yet those student affairs organizations that plan effectively are able to defuse efforts to reduce their funding (Deegan

1981). More concerted planning in student affairs is necessary if it is to be proactive.

A model for comprehensive planning suggested by Schroeder (1975) is the basis of a planning model for the student affairs unit developed by Biggs and Skinner (1979). Schroeder outlines a three-track planning system in which the tracks are interrelated and demand simultaneous development. The first of these tracks is the *definition of a planning process*—one that defines how planning will be undertaken, assigns responsibility for planning, and outlines a planning calendar. The second track is the *development of plans for the division* and its units. This track involves the assessment of the current situation, clarification of goal statements, and the means for achievement. The third track is the *development of a planning information system* to support the planning process.

Long-range planning in student affairs is the management of change and is a method that enables student personnel administrators to prepare for the future.

> *Long-range planning is not difficult, but [it] demands a good deal of thought as well as innovation; it is a process [that] does not necessarily provide solutions to all problems, but when applied, can aid administrators in making rational decisions from among available choices* (Priest, Alphenaar, and Boer 1980, p. 7).

While experts do not agree as to which planning model or process is most appropriate for the student affairs organization, it remains a critical skill area, for through effective planning, student affairs will be able to meet the challenges of its future.

Management information systems. To plan and manage more effectively and to become more knowledgeable about student trends, student affairs organizations need more usable information about students, staff, and their programs and services in the form of a management information system. Such a system performs several important tasks—planning, program evaluation, budgeting and budgetary control, organizing and storing large amounts of information, providing up-to-date information on the condition of the organization, and providing a mechanism for modeling and simulating (Racippo and

Foxley 1980). Most student affairs organizations collect or use too little information; the collection and dissemination of information is rarely consistent and systematic, often gathered in response to specific, ad hoc requests (Benezet 1979). If student affairs organizations are to plan more effectively, to translate students' needs into programs and services, and to be truly knowledgeable when communicating with other divisions of the institution, the effective management of information is imperative (University of Minnesota 1981). Student affairs management information systems must combine both quantitative and qualitative information about programs, students, and staff (Casper and Morey 1976).

Student affairs organizations have access to various sources of information about students, staff, facilities, financing, and curricula with which they can design, justify, or reorganize programs and services for increased effectiveness and efficiency (Racippo and Foxley 1980, p. 69). A management information system should be designed to allow student affairs organizations to take advantage of those information sources and, by doing so, plan and manage more effectively.

Related to skills in the development and application of management information systems are computer and information-processing skills. Increasingly, opportunities are available for the employment of computers in student affairs for purposes ranging from monitoring students' achievement to computerized career guidance systems. Personal computers and access to campus main-frame computers allow student affairs professionals to computerize and analyze student records, admission records, financial aid information, housing assignments, and, as a result, opportunities for research are increasing. The management of computer resources is an emerging issue for student affairs (Sampson 1982).

Financial management skills. As with many other skills, student personnel preparation programs rarely devote much effort to the development of resource management skills at the master's degree level, yet student affairs administrators at all levels are increasingly asked to become familiar with the budgeting process. Much of this change occurs as a result of the increasing application of planning and management models to higher education. A study of four institutions facing retrenchment concluded that student affairs administrators need greater budgeting skills as a result of the loss of budget flexibility and the increase in budget controls and that more training should be given in budget techniques, procedures, and politics (Deegan 1981).

Effective resource management depends upon more than technical competency and political skills; it also depends on finding answers to pertinent questions about costs and programs: (1) What do programs cost in terms of funds and personnel? (2) What is their purpose, intended clientele, and frequency of use? (3) How effective are they? (4) What other delivery mechanisms could be employed? (5) What is the best configuration for the use of staff and resources to meet the goals of the division and the institution? Such questions are essential to efforts designed to result in the more effective use of staff.

Human resource management. Student affairs staffs, in the broadest sense, are comprised of full- and part-time professionals, full- and part-time paraprofessionals, and faculty and administrators contributing on a part-time basis. Managing these resources—which are the strengths of student affairs— is increasingly important. The efficiency of the use of staff, training and supervision, professional development, and the identification and assignment of responsibility for tasks are all issues in the management of human resources. With attention to human development skills in preparation programs, many student affairs professionals possess the underlying skills, but their further development is often needed for the professionals to become more effective at human resource management (Johnson and Foxley 1980).

Related management skills. Administrators in student affairs should also possess skills in goal setting and time management (Johnson and Foxley 1980). Time management skills are essential to planning activities, and they are essential if student affairs professionals are to be able to capture the time to become more centrally involved in the institution (Abel 1978). To that end, leaders must act on targets that yield the greatest educational output and terminate unneeded functions, delegating and redesigning jobs to use and expand the talents of others (Abel 1978).

Political skills

An uncertain situation, largely caused by scarce resources and new student clienteles, heightens competition among vested interests seeking to protect their positions in the institution. Rational planning models to the contrary, institutional politics are involved in establishing priorities, developing budgets, and formulating strategies to respond to changing conditions. To participate in that atmosphere and to promote the position of student affairs in providing leadership within the institution, the student affairs administrator must possess political and diplomatic skills to bring about change and to gain power and influence (Abel 1978; Shaffer 1973). These skills are particularly important if student affairs professionals are to be effective advocates for students and their profession.

While management skills allow administrators to assume authority based on managerial position, political skills allow them to extend their influence beyond their formal authority. This involves the ability to influence colleagues, mobilize support, and remove barriers (Abel 1978, p. 239).

Student affairs leaders should become more aware of institutional politics to promote student affairs efforts in times of reduction (Deegan 1981). Through an understanding of the institution and employment of political skills within that setting, student affairs leaders might be able to assist in developing the potential of the institution to meet changing conditions.

As "leading edge" administrators, student affairs professionals can be instrumental in integrating the goals of various interest groups within the institution (faculty, students, administrators) and help forge policy decisions reflecting that integration (Silverman 1980). The relationship between the chief student affairs officer and the president is critical to the political position of student affairs; to the extent that the president and the student affairs officer share goals and an understanding of the institution, the more politically secure will be the student affairs organization (Shay 1984).

To that end, student personnel professionals should develop power networks as a base for developing support on specific issues, become aware of manipulative strategies, and use their human relations skills to build a collaborative environment for negotiation and bargaining (Abel 1978). To do so will require the application of the student affairs professional's human relations skills coupled with a greater understanding of the institution and the people within it.

Research and evaluation skills

If student affairs administrators are to become effective and knowledgeable leaders in this period of change, they will have to develop and apply research and evaluation skills. Research on students is necessary to develop student affairs programs, to modify existing programs, and to justify the efforts of student affairs if student affairs professionals are to solidify their position within the institutions. Effective handling of complex issues requires usable information from a variety of sources (Shaffer 1973).

Research is costly in terms of time and money, even more so in a period when both are so precious. In some institutions facing retrenchment, however, the student affairs organization with an established research unit has been able to justify its programs and serve as a resource for other university decision makers (Deegan 1981). A recent study of research activities in student affairs organizations found that 85 percent of institutions surveyed conducted research at least occasionally, largely focusing on program evaluation, needs assessment, and characteristics of students (Johnson and Steele 1984). While this research was valuable to decision makers in student affairs, however, few efforts were made to put the findings of research to use in institutional decisions (Johnson and Steele 1984).

Research could be useful to student affairs administrators in several areas:

- *Longitudinal studies of students—their decision-making processes, values, interests, needs, changes over time, and the impacts of college on their development.*
- *More research on high school students, . . . including studies of academic ability, values, interests, needs, and expectations about college.*

- *Studies to assist counselors, such as research on changing job markets or career counseling techniques.*
- *Studies on factors that attract students to the college and on factors that increase retention rates at the college (including those student affairs efforts [that] contribute to retention).*
- *Periodic studies of student[s'] interests, preferences, needs, and opinions about life at the college and suggestions for change.*
- *Management studies for program evaluation. . .* (Deegan 1981, pp. 219–20).

In collaboration with faculty and institutional researchers, student affairs leaders will be able to become more knowledgeable and influential within the campus community.

Organizational skills

If student affairs administrators are going to serve as integrators within institutions, they must possess a well-developed understanding of the institution and society in addition to their own organization. They will, quite simply, need to develop a broad perspective and understanding of student affairs and its relationship to the institution.

Several authors have recently discussed the importance of organizational understanding to the future of student affairs. Kuh (1983, 1984) proposes a perspective on student affairs organizations based on an integration of traditional perspectives (including the collegial, political, and bureaucratic). More broadly, student affairs organizations must more clearly understand and address institutional goals in developing their goals: "Student affairs, if it is to be effective and successful, must see itself as part of an institution and supportive of institutional mission" (Smith 1982, p. 56). Student affairs professionals in larger institutions could learn much from their colleagues in smaller institutions (Palm 1984). There, student affairs staff are more connected with other professionals and possess a broader and more complete understanding of the institution. If student development is going to truly become an institutional goal, then student affairs professionals must expand their knowledge of the institutional environment and develop skills for working within that environment (Borland and Thomas 1976).

Understanding the institution of which student affairs is a part is very important (Smith 1982). The nature of most academic programs is content-bound and cognitively based, emphasizing the mind. Most student affairs programs, on the other hand, define development more holistically by also emphasizing social, emotional, and physical development. To capture the interest and attention of faculty, however, student affairs philosophies must be stated in terms that academic leaders are able to understand and justify. Communicating that philosophy to academic leaders entails the use of highly developed skills, of which an enlightened understanding of the institution and its environment is an essential part.

To better understand the institution in which they seek to become full partners, student affairs professionals should incorporate the following elements in their approach (Smith 1982, p. 59). First, they must identify with their colleagues outside of student affairs to better understand them and their priorities; they must develop credibility and respectability in the eyes of their academic partners. Second, if it is assumed that members of an organization should share goals, student affairs professionals must be sensitive to the relationship of their programs to the rest of the institution. Third, student affairs must understand the environment in which it operates the organizational culture, decision-making patterns, and formal and informal organizational structure. To do so, it must assess the organizations of which it is part. An organizational assessment should encompass the following elements: (1) an evaluation of job descriptions and of roles related to others in the organization; (2) a determination of role expectations by those affecting the positions of student affairs; (3) a determination of power in decision making; and (4) goals for student affairs as defined by others (Borland and Thomas 1976).

To those who would say that student affairs professionals are novices in understanding the institutions of which they are part and in the game of institutional politics, that marginality and naiveté may be hidden strengths; student affairs professionals are in a desirable position to create and nurture significant links in loosely coupled systems

(Silverman 1980). That improved position will come, however, only as student affairs better understands the institutions and society of which it is a part.

Implications for Programs and Services

A changing role for student affairs and similar changes in
the role of the chief student affairs officer have implications for the programs and activities conducted by student
affairs organizations. Students' demands will argue for certain programs to be developed or enhanced or deempha-
sized; similarly, changing institutional emphases will
enhance some efforts and question the need for others.
Among those efforts likely to be emphasized in the 1980s
are recruitment and retention, the integration of nontraditional student clienteles, and career planning and placement and services for students; those likely to be deem-
phasized include student activities in which students
express little interest and the development of values. And,
finally, certain programs and services deemed essential by
student affairs staff, but no longer popular with institutional leaders or students, will need to be repackaged to
make them attractive to changed or to different student
groups.

These changes have implications for the various traditional functional areas of student affairs (residence halls,
financial aid, student activities, for example); more important, they will create opportunities for general responses
from student affairs, including advising, counseling, and
retention. Moreover, the potential exists within these
activities for team efforts, including other administrators
and faculty.

Recruitment and retention

Efforts in recruitment and retention include advising, counseling, developing and maintaining a supportive campus
environment, orientation programs, and timely and adequate financial aid programs, and they involve preadmission programs, academic and social orientation programs,
visible and well-advertised campus services, faculty outreach and advising, student activities, and housing. Generally, they are the support services that enhance the retention of students through social integration. They call on the

traditional expertise of student affairs staff mixed with a special insight into the needs of today's students.

A study of the projected effects of enrollment and budget reductions on student personnel programs found that funds for recruitment and retention programs and services—including financial aid, support services for nontraditional students, and minority recruitment—were projected to remain unchanged (Nelson and Murphy 1980). Similarly, enrollment/retention efforts and recruitment programs would be established and expanded.

The expanded use of enrollment management involving faculty and student affairs is also important to recruitment and retention. Faculty and student affairs professionals must work together to integrate students' social and emotional needs, academic expectations and achievement, and institutional goals, with the ultimate goal being to improve the recruitment and retention of students (Baldridge, Kemerer, and Green 1982).

Nontraditional students

Increasing participation in higher education by a variety of groups exhibiting different ethnic and racial backgrounds, levels of preparation, age, motivation, and interest in attending college has placed and will continue to place demands on student affairs staff. The ability to provide new services or to modify existing services to meet these new demands will be essential if student affairs and institutions are to promote individual development as a professional goal and to maintain enrollments as an institutional goal.

Programs and services for special populations—returning adults, women, commuting/part-time, minority, and disabled students—might include support centers for special populations, special orientation programs, academic and personal counseling, and learning assistance for basic skills. The potential of faculty and student affairs staff working together in these areas creates a significant opportunity for the expansion of joint efforts.

Institutions are likely to continue funding such programs and services as special services for handicapped students, facilities for older or married students, academic advising, learning assistance centers, and special services for international students and women (Nelson and Murphy 1980). In each of these areas, the potential exists for teams of student affairs professionals, faculty, administrators, and other professionals to be increasingly involved in coordinated, comprehensive efforts aimed at the needs of nontraditional students.

Career-oriented activities

Increasing vocationalism among students suggests an enlarged role for career planning and placement and related activities throughout the institution. Students are increasingly concerned about selecting careers, involving themselves in those courses and activities that will enhance their attractiveness to prospective employers. As such, career planning and placement will be priorities for most student affairs organizations. With placement in positions after graduation being an important element in the attraction of students, career planning and placement efforts are important to institutional goals.

Reflecting this trend, academic enhancement programs, career planning and placement activities, and career-oriented student activities are among programs gaining visibility in institutions. It should come as no surprise, then, when career counseling and placement offices, programs, and services receive priority in institutional and departmental budgets (Nelson and Murphy 1980). At Montana State University, for example, several new programs were initiated, including a liberal arts career internship program, alumni career networks, and career planning workshops for freshmen and sophomores.

Computerized systems

Computerized financial accounting systems and computer-based career planning and placement services are services likely to be established in light of changing conditions (Nelson and Murphy 1980). Similarly, the role of computerized management and guidance systems will grow in student affairs, partially as a result of new technologies and partly as a result of decreased funds for personnel. Examples abound of the reliance on electronic data processing in student affairs—monitoring the progress of underprepared students at the University of Georgia, evaluating student affairs programs at the University of Nebraska, and evaluating student activities at the Community College of Allegheny County.

Student activities in trouble

The study by Nelson and Murphy (1980) does not project a bright future for student activities. Of the 22 services, programs, and functions projected to be reduced, 12 were in the realm of student activities, including Greek affairs, student government, academic clubs, student media, and student entertainment programs. This result should be expected, given observations about students' decreasing interest in community service activities and political issues and an increase in personal activities and career and interest groups (Levine 1980). Those activities most directly associated with a successful career are likely to be most popular (Astin 1984a).

Participation in student activities contributes to a student's involvement in college life and is a powerful predictor of student retention and satisfaction with college (Astin 1984b). But it is important to note that many student activities are directed toward the traditional college student, now a minority of those attending colleges and universities. The importance of student activities, coupled with students' decreasing interest, suggests that student activities as they are currently offered must be repackaged to retain students' interest.

The development of values

The development of values is inextricably bound to the development of a student, and commitment to one presupposes commitment to the other (Thomas, Murrell, and Chickering 1982). The student affairs professional is in a unique position to shape students' moral or value development. Efforts at values education, built on a firm theoretical foundation, can provide guidance to student affairs professionals who would seek to develop values in students (Kohlberg 1969; Perry 1970).

While professional interest in the development of values remains, students are less actively interested in developing a personal philosophy, exploring values, and engaging in activities that express social concern (political parties and community service activities, for example) (Astin and others 1984; Levine 1980). Thus, students may not seek to avail themselves of opportunities to challenge and develop values, and student affairs efforts aimed at moral education or the development of values will need to be more aggressive to engage students. Student affairs professionals should seek to maximize those areas—residence halls, student groups, and student activities—where the development of values typically occurs (Thomas, Murrell, and Chickering 1982). Further, programs aimed at the development of values may need to directly address students' current interests and expressed needs. For instance, values may have to be explored as an element of educational and career expectations (that is, with a goal of integrating career goals and personal values).

Summary
Changing conditions have several implications for student affairs (Nelson and Murphy 1980). First, long-range planning is necessary to deal effectively with changing conditions and students. Second, programs that aid in student retention should be developed and emphasized. Third, administrators should examine each student affairs program to determine whether it is operating at the best cost/benefit ratio; such an examination may lead to the improvement of services without increased expenditures. Fourth, and perhaps most important, student affairs professionals should routinely survey the needs of their students to determine the relative importance of each student service program or function.

Greater attention must be paid to the needs of educational consumers (Aiken 1982). A routine analysis of needs would permit administrators to retain, consolidate, or curtail programs on the basis of their contribution to students' needs.

This review of probable changes in student affairs suggests that many of those efforts that cut across the traditional student affairs functional areas—for example, retention and attention to the needs of nontraditional students—will receive increased attention because of their importance as institutional priorities. In addition, these student affairs efforts are encouraging others in the institution, an important outcome in itself. To the extent that those activities in which student affairs engages support institutional goals, great potential exists for student affairs professionals to lead other administrators and faculty in the development of efforts leading to individual development and efforts supporting institutional or organizational development. Integrating the institution's and students' needs suggests an enhanced, more central role for student affairs professionals.

EDUCATING STUDENT PERSONNEL PROFESSIONALS

In addition to the traditional *interpersonal* skills of student affairs professionals, the new role demands new *organizational* skills—planning and management, resource management, research and evaluation, and political skills. Likewise, to the extent that student development provides a theoretical basis for the profession, a greater awareness of the organizational context for student development and the skills necessary for working effectively within that context are needed. These new skills are critical if student affairs professionals are to be able to integrate students' and institutions' needs meaningfully.

Preparation programs for student personnel professionals, however, devote little effort to organizational skills (Arner et al. 1977; Delworth, Hanson, and associates 1980; Knock 1977). They tend to focus on counseling skills and often neglect attention to the needs of new student groups (Wright 1984). A more visible, central role for student affairs does not diminish the need for counseling skills, but it demands skills in dealing with people and situations outside the student affairs office. A significant redirection of preparation programs for student personnel professionals, supplemented by ongoing professional development, is critical to the new role for student affairs and its future.

Preparation Programs

Today, a number of issues in the preparation of student personnel professionals are heightened by changing conditions and students. Among these issues are attention to organizational skills and addressing new student subpopulations, an understanding and commitment to student development, and expected entry-level competencies.

The curriculum of a professional preparation program has several aims: (1) to set professional standards; (2) to assess current status and facilitate change in the profession; (3) to select and manage staff; and (4) to establish academic legitimacy (Delworth, Hanson, and associates 1980). A curriculum that prepares people to enter the field, in short, is one important way that a profession defines itself. Little agreement is evident in the literature, however, over the appropriate goals, competencies, and form that a curriculum for the preparation of student personnel professionals should take, partly the result of the diverse functions performed by student affairs professionals. More

A curriculum that prepares people to enter the field, in short, is one important way that a profession defines itself.

important, it is the applied nature of the field, which borrows from many other disciplines, theories, and philosophies, that contributes to the confusion. The field is still searching for a guiding philosophy that would in part help it to define the general skills and competencies appropriate for entry into the field (Stamatakos and Rogers 1984).

Although the content of programs in student personnel has received much attention, many of the models seek only to better prepare counselors (Arner et al. 1977; Knock 1977; Pruitt 1979; Spooner 1979). Delworth, Hanson, and associates (1980) provide an example of a well-developed curriculum that focuses on preparing entry-level student affairs professionals. Their improved curriculum for the training of student affairs professionals consists of several core components:

1. History and philosophy of the field and of higher education.
2. Theory—one course concerned with theories of human development and one course concerned with theories of person/environment interaction.
3. Models of practice and role orientation, covered in one course concerned with patterns of organization and specialized functions in student services.
4. Core competencies—one course covering each area (assessment and evaluation, consultation, instruction, and counseling).
5. Specialized competencies—at least one course in this area, covering program development, environmental assessment, and paraprofessional training.
6. Administration and management—a basic course focused on the management tools needed by the entry-level professional.
7. Practicum or field work—a one-year practicum in at least two student service areas.
8. Additional theory and tool courses (pp. 481–82).

While attention to theory in the model would serve to increase the credibility of the profession and further encourage the application of student development, little attention is given to the development of organizational skills. Much confusion surrounds the topic because little attempt is made to distinguish between professional roles, target or clientele groups to be addressed, and the competencies needed to carry out these roles (Morrill 1980). Training the student development specialist for the roles of diagnostician, consultant, programmer, technologist, professor, behavioral scientist, and administrator is important (Brown 1972), just as is training in group processes, organization and administration, measurement and evaluation, and counseling theory (Pruitt 1979).

Preparation programs that take into consideration the changes in the student body should be included in the design of curricula (Pruitt 1979). These clienteles and approaches for training include women (including the psychology and sociology of women's development, elimination of stereotyping, and the like), nonwhite persons (including the history and culture of this segment of the population and professional and institutional racism), and disabled students (including the psychology and sociology of their development). In addition to infusing coursework with content in the areas of sex equity, nonwhite concerns, and mainstreaming of the handicapped, disabled and minority group members should be recruited into the profession (Pruitt 1979).

While attention to organizational skills is infrequently offered, the development of skills that add credibility to the profession, promote academic respectability, and enhance working relationships between faculty and student affairs is even more rarely addressed. These skills include research, teaching, and scholarship. Student affairs does not have a strong tradition of preparing researchers, scholars, and teachers (in the traditional sense), but if, as professionals, their goals are to be accepted by faculty, they must develop and use those skills.

Preparation for Administration and Management
Despite the fact that many leaders in student affairs have advocated increased management skills (see, for example, Aery and Moore 1976; Biggs and Skinner 1979; Deegan 1981; Kuh 1981; Priest, Alphenaar, and Boer 1980; Racippo and Foxley 1980), research and evaluation skills (Deegan 1981), political skills (Abel 1978; Deegan 1981), and organizational understanding (Borland 1980) to meet the challenge of changing conditions, models for educating student personnel professionals rarely attend to these skills

in preparation programs. For instance, the program proposed by Delworth, Hanson, and associates (1980) includes only one course on basic management skills appropriate for the entry-level worker, even though management skills may be more important to the professional than human development skills (Kuh 1981).

It can be argued that management, organizational, and political skills are most necessary for chief student personnel officers and that, for those who provide primary service, increased attention to management skills might even prove counterproductive. The numbers of administrators and managers in student affairs as well as the numbers of those who aspire to the higher levels of the profession, however, suggest that greater attention should be given to management and organizational skills for professionals at all levels. It is of some concern where and when these skills are to be developed. Perhaps it is the role of doctoral programs in which student affairs professionals are trained to enter institutions as academic leaders (Bloland 1979), but a recent study of chief student affairs officers found that only half possessed doctorates and of that group, 20 percent held degrees in higher education administration (Ostroth, Efird, and Lerman 1984). This finding perhaps indicates that student affairs leaders desire greater attention to the development of administrative and organizational skills.

Further, if it is assumed that the graduate curriculum reflects the needs of the profession and its concerns, current curricula suggest that the profession remains more interested in human relations skills and student development competencies than in the organizational skills necessary for the institutionalization of the changes student development advocates. The lack of attention to management and organizational skills is most surprising when one realizes that a guiding student development model for the field (Miller and Prince 1977) is predicated on the fact that student development professionals will be able to modify institutional goals and practices to conform with the goals of student development, yet little effort is made to address the development of skills necessary for the accomplishment of that goal. A changing role argues for student affairs professionals with the specialized skills in the area of human development enhanced by those skills demanded by working in complex organizations and systems.

Entry-level Competencies

A survey of student personnel administrators who hired entry-level staff found several specific skill areas particularly important in the selection of staff: (1) competency in assessing students' needs and interests; (2) competency in mediating conflicts between individuals and groups; (3) competency in group advisement and in recognition of group dynamics; and (4) competency in programming (Ostroth 1981). Among the least important competencies reported in the survey were familiarity with professional literature, the ability to articulate and interpret the goals of student personnel work to the wider population, an understanding of the financing of higher education, the ability to formulate and monitor budgets, and the ability to recognize and analyze political processes in higher education. In short, the skill areas required to work directly with students were rated most important, those necessary to understand and work with the remainder of the institution least important.

Seventy-three percent of chief student affairs officers believe preparation programs to be good or excellent (Sandeen 1982). A paradox is thereby suggested by these studies of expected competencies for the profession—the training priorities and curricula discussed in the literature on the one hand, and the skills outlined by leaders in the field as necessary for effective student affairs professionals and for the enhancement of the student affairs profession on the other. The former argues for skills relevant to working with students, the latter for skills necessary for working within organizations. It can be argued that it is the chief personnel officer who interacts most frequently with other university administrators and faculty and that these organizational skills are therefore not necessary for entry-level workers. But this situation raises two questions. First, if all student personnel professionals are presumed to be working with others in the institutional setting, should they not possess, to some degree, organizational skills? Second, presuming that most entry-level workers aspire to advancement within the profession, at what point do they learn those organizational skills that allow them to become effective administrators?

A New Model for Professional Preparation
A recently proposed content and process model seeks to prepare student development educators with a greater understanding of the system of which they are a part (Brown 1985b). That model is a significant departure from previous models, and as such, it provides a model for graduate education that recognizes and is compatible with the changing role of student affairs.

In lieu of focusing almost exclusively on students, the model would have student affairs professionals also focus on themselves and on the institutional system, the latter of which is most critical to the preparation of those who will be institutional integrators. Program development does not take place in a vacuum.

> *[It] occurs [rather] within a highly interactive system. New professionals need to understand the history and philosophy of that system, possess knowledge of how organizations function and change, and understand the effects of individual interaction with the organizational environment. In practice, this means understanding the essentials of management theory, budgeting, organizational and staff development, environmental assessment, and program evaluation. Internships and practicums should provide students with the opportunity to plan, implement, and evaluate programs* (Brown 1985b, p. 39).

Brown's model is based on several guiding principles:

1. *The goal of higher education is to foster total student development, including . . . intellectual, aesthetic, physical, spiritual, interpersonal . . . , and cultural awareness.*
2. *Nonintellectual dimensions of development need to be integrated with traditional academic intellectual dimensions.*
3. *The scientist/practitioner role provides a useful goal for program development for graduate program content and process.*

4. *The following areas of knowledge form core cognates for the student development educator: learning theory, ethics, human development theory, research design, theories of organizational behavior, and management theory.*
5. *The program should prepare generalists through course work. Training related to specific student affairs agencies and functions can be provided through practicum[s] and internship[s]. . . .*
6. *The program should emulate the ideals [of] higher education in general through its . . . focus on total development of [the] student with emphasis on professional development and . . . [its] inclusion of a process that involves students in planning their personal and professional growth. . .* (Brown 1985b, pp. 40–41).

The model, though it does not specify courses, does specify areas for attention in the preparation of programs (see table 2, p. 96). And it is those areas, already outlined, that are demanded by a changing role for student affairs.

Continuing Professional Education
Graduate education, while critical to the preparation of professionals for the changing role of student affairs, is not the only route by which professionals can become more prepared to meet the challenges of their new role. Another route is continuing professional education.

Professional development, staff development, and in-service education—the ongoing activities that seek to enhance or improve the skills and competencies of professionals to meet the challenges of their position in an assertive, productive fashion (Cox and Ivy 1984)—are not new to student affairs. They are still in their infancy, however (Hall 1981). Professional development activities until recently tended to be sporadic, reactive, and aimed at practical solutions to immediate concerns, but they have become more formal in-service programs at some institutions (Canon 1984; Hall 1981). Despite the importance of professional development for the future of the profession, professional development in student affairs often lacks a coherent plan (Shaffer 1984).

TABLE 2
GRADUATE EDUCATION PROGRAM MODEL FOR STUDENT
DEVELOPMENT EDUCATORS

Self	Students	Systems

Learning Level I: Basic Knowledge

Self	Students	Systems
Self-assessment Strategies Total Development— intellectual, academic, interpersonal, aesthetic, physical, spiritual	Learning Theory Developmental Theory Vocational Theory	Organizational Behavior History and Philosophy of Higher Education History and Philosophy of Student Affairs Person/Environment Theory

Learning Level II: Program Prescription Blended with Self-assessment and Negotiation

Self	Students	Systems
Personal Goal Setting Strategies for Personal Change	Counseling Practices (one- to-one consulting group) Instructional Strategies	Management/Budgeting Consulting Organizational Development Program Evaluation Research Design Staff Development

Learning Level III: Experiential Learning (synthesis and evaluation)

Self	Students	Systems
Mentoring Relationship with Advisor	Teaching Counseling/Consulting Program Planning Mentoring Group Work	Internship in Consulting, Evaluation, Research

Source: Brown 1985b, p. 41.

The reasons for offering a professional development program are varied: (1) the remediation of marginally trained or skilled professionals; (2) the enhancement of accountability to institutions for the work of student affairs professionals; and (3) ensuring professional growth (Canon 1984). Efforts aimed at the remediation of staff are made in response to the diverse backgrounds, professional preparations, and outlooks new or entering professionals bring with them. New roles within institutions and attention to diverse student clienteles argue for professional development on a wide variety of topics, including awareness of various minority populations and management skills. And, finally, professional growth includes training to ensure the development of professional organizations as well as individuals (Carpenter and Miller 1981).

A recent study of the professional development needs of student affairs professionals revealed that the top five needs were for organizational skills and that they included communicating program goals to the larger academic community, collaborating with faculty and other administrators, and obtaining the respect of academicians (Cox and Ivy 1984). Interestingly, respondents indicated little need to improve skills required in working with students, such as general counseling and communications. Thus, special emphasis in professional development programs is needed to impart strategies for enhancing the relationship between student affairs and academic affairs: (1) using faculty expertise in student affairs professional development; (2) becoming more visible and recognized; and (3) developing experiences—such as seminar series—on which to collaborate (Cox and Ivy 1984). This study suggests that student affairs professionals desire enhanced skills in working with other administrators and faculty in addition to a greater understanding of their environment.

Professional development activities are typically part-time, campus-based responses to the educational needs of student affairs staff. Continuing professional education encompasses far more, however. Individual and group participation in courses, degree and nondegree programs, and national, regional, and state associations and conferences all allow student affairs staff to continue their professional development beyond the campus.

For student affairs leaders, another route to the development of skills appropriate to an enhanced role is the growing number of higher education management programs, including Harvard's Institute for Educational Management and Bryn Mawr's summer program for women in higher education. These programs provide leaders with a variety of backgrounds the opportunity to develop greater management and organizational skills.

Regardless of the structure or method, continuing professional education is increasingly important for student affairs professionals, and national student affairs associations and institutions should develop comprehensive plans that seek to develop skills appropriate for new roles.

Summary

A new role for student affairs demands new and enhanced skills for professionals. As such, it places special demands on graduate education for the profession. Existing preparation programs need to be revised in light of the expanding role for student affairs. Similarly, continuing professional education must address the ongoing needs for new and enhanced skills. New efforts in graduate preparation and continuing professional education are critical, not only to the fulfillment of a challenging new role but also to the future vitality of the profession.

In light of new roles for student affairs, therefore, efforts must be made to restructure preparation programs and to develop continuing professional education to:

1. Attend more to management skills, research and evaluation skills, and a better understanding of organizational behavior and development;
2. Address the needs of diverse student populations;
3. Create a greater awareness among professionals of societal trends, higher education issues, and institutional responses that demand enlightened responses from student affairs; and
4. Develop those skills—research, teaching, and scholarship—through which the profession will be able to increase its credibility within the institution.

THE CHALLENGES OF STUDENT DEVELOPMENT

Student development in its many forms—guiding philosophy, formal theory, and model for action—has served to give meaning and direction to the student affairs function (American Council on Education 1938; Brown 1972; Council of Student Personnel Associations 1975; Williamson 1949). At the same time, student development, in a general sense, typically is cited as one of the goals of most institutions; as a priority, however, student development has rarely received the attention that has been given to cognitive development nor the amount of attention that student affairs professionals would desire (Miller and Prince 1977). While many forces are at work to drive institutions to a greater acceptance of student development (Harvey 1976), institutional budgets suggest that the student development function has eroded on many campuses (Deegan 1981; Harpel 1975). Furthermore, as the theoretical basis of the profession, student development is being challenged on many fronts.

. . . As the theoretical basis of the profession, student development is being challenged on many fronts.

All of which is to say that if student development is to remain an integrating concept for the profession and is to serve to undergird the efforts of student affairs professionals as they become institutional integrators, then several issues must be addressed. First, for student development to succeed, a greater understanding and acceptance of student development theory must be gained within the profession. Second, student development theory must be expanded to embrace what we know about the needs of changing student clienteles. And third, student development and administrative practice must be integrated, and both must serve the goal of organizational development.

A Theoretical Basis for the Profession

The adoption and application of theory is important to a professional field. A theoretical basis for the student affairs profession allows us to accomplish several important tasks (Delworth, Hanson, and associates 1980). First, it helps student affairs professionals to organize information. Second, it helps them explain to others what they do. Third, it aids professional decisions. And, fourth, it helps student affairs staff to guide future efforts as much as present efforts. Further, basing student affairs practice on a systematic body of knowledge in the form of theory helps the field to define itself as a profession.

Student development has been defined as "the application of human development concepts in postsecondary settings so that everyone can master increasingly complex developmental tasks, achieve self-direction, and become interdependent" (Miller and Prince 1977, p. 3). As such, student development is not a single theory but a collection of theories and concepts concerned with human development.

Adoption and Application of Theory

Recent studies indicate that developmental theory is not well understood by many in the profession, and student development programming does not appear to reflect theories promoted by various student personnel professional organizations (Kuh et al. 1977). Furthermore, the knowledge of student development theory within the profession and its application in practice are not widespread (Strange and Contomanolis 1983).

In place of formal theory, many student affairs staff "probably use informal, internally consistent but, for the most part, unexamined 'theories in action' to guide their work with students" (Kuh 1981, p. 30). Similarly, informal theories tend to guide efforts more than formal theories, perhaps because student personnel professionals are practical service providers (Widick, Knefelkamp, and Parker 1980).

Professionals typically possess some informal student development theory that guides their actions, even if their knowledge and application of formal theories is less widespread. Three strategies would help promote the use and application of formal theory in practice:

1. Using formal theory in working with broad conceptual issues at the level of the college.
2. Combining elements of formal and informal theory in working with groups of relatively homogenous students.
3. Using informal theories to understand and apply the research findings from formal theories (Widick, Knefelkamp, and Parker 1980, pp. 112–13).

The practicality of applying theory in the practice of student development has been demonstrated.

When the theory is made actual with real people involved, a data base is generated that provides a con-

crete base for defining and understanding the problem in the real setting, and provides a basis for defining appropriate content and developmental goals and objectives. Finally, theories also provide criteria for designing developmentally appropriate interventions and for defining and measuring outcomes (Rodgers 1982, p. 140).

For numerous reasons, continued efforts to organize and disseminate knowledge about student development are essential to the future of student affairs. First, if student affairs professionals are to continue in efforts to develop students as well as their own professionalism, they should accomplish those goals through efforts grounded in developmental theory, not solely through the trial and error of previous experience. Second, in a practical sense, a theoretical justification coupled with expressed consumer interest can establish a stronger argument for the support of student affairs. And, third, a well-understood theoretical base is important to the establishment of credibility and respectability as a profession in the eyes of faculty. This last point is particularly important if student affairs professionals are to be able to integrate student and academic life as well as institutional and student goals.

Incorporating Diverse Clienteles
Another challenge of student development suggests broadening student development theory to encompass the needs of increasing minority subpopulations enrolling in colleges and universities. Although these students face different developmental issues because of their age, sex, level of preparation, or cultural backgrounds, much of the current student development theory emerged from studies of traditional white male college students at small residential institutions, and one cannot be assured of their appropriateness for different students. Student affairs professionals must continue to identify appropriate applications and discover the limitations of theories and models currently in practice. In some cases, a return to human development theory and the exploration of issues of development for older students and women students is warranted (Cross 1981a; Erikson 1963; Weathersby and Tarule 1980), while in other cases, different cultural contexts for human development must be examined (Vasquez and Chavez 1980). Current student

development theories should not be discarded but must be carefully reviewed and tested for applicability with the various subgroups that make up increasing minority student subpopulations.

For instance, what comprises student development in the future should incorporate an understanding of adult development. While some traditional student development issues are important for adults, different issues emerge for adult students as a result of different life stages (Greenfeig and Goldberg 1984). The various life-cycle stages through which adults pass offer challenges and opportunities (Levinson and others 1978). Adults are characterized by life phases with a variety of development issues characterizing each, and institutions should be aware of them and seek to address them in programs and services (Weathersby and Tarule 1980).

Integration with Administrative Practice

Perhaps the clearest challenge for student development theory is its integration with administrative practice in colleges and universities. Student development theory implies the development of students as the guiding principle for student affairs organizations, but these organizations are also units of institutions that have related but usually different goals and priorities. Formulating responses to changing conditions, student affairs organizations must be attentive to both students' and institutions' needs; they must be responsive to students and to systems. If student affairs professionals are to be integrators, then they must attempt to foster institutional or organizational development as well as student development (Borland 1980).

To the extent that the profession has become focused on student development and neglected institutional goals, it has become increasingly peripheral. Others in the institution have rarely embraced student development practices. The goals of institutions and student affairs are often not integrated, and student development has not been incorporated into administrative or academic practice.

Very seldom is institutional mission or identification with mission referred to in the literature on student development (Smith 1982). Even Miller and Prince's model (1977), which discusses environmental strategies, concentrates on the goals of the model and their applicability to the institution, neglecting the importance of institutional goals. Furthermore, the barriers to organizational change are considerable (Borland 1980; Strange 1981). As a result, for student development to be viable as a cornerstone of student affairs, more attention must be given "to the supportive properties of institutions that support innovations or changes in practice such as student development programs" (Kuh 1981, p. 29).

Current financial and enrollment problems argue for the preservation of the institution, but not necessarily for student affairs (Strange 1981). That is, unless a convincing argument for the importance of student development to the institution is made, the student affairs profession may be threatened. Put simply, student development must become more institutional and the institution must become more student developmental if both are to remain viable.

A view of student affairs that is to have legitimacy and credibility today must demonstrate an understanding of the goals of the institution, its intellectual and academic missions, and its needs for organizational development. A view incorporating these elements holds great promise for students, institutions, and the profession (Borland 1980; Shaffer 1973; Smith 1982).

In short, changing conditions may create an environment where an active student affairs organization can use its expertise to promote the development of both students and institutions, different but parallel goals. If student affairs professionals are to capitalize on opportunities to become institutional integrators, then student and organizational development should become similarly integrated. Organizational development is a conscious effort to improve the internal capabilities of an organization to cope with the demands of external environments; as such, it shares many components with student development.

> *Organization development is a theoretical and a practical concept for improving the effectiveness and efficiency of an institution. Student development is a concept within the student affairs profession that promotes an institutional environment conducive to and facilitative of the human development of students. . . . [T]he two concepts are inseparable* (Borland 1980, p. 223).

A New Theory of Development

Responding to what he sees as chaos in the literature, Astin (1984b) proposes a theory of student involvement as a developmental theory for higher education. Student involvement refers to the amount of physical and psychological energy that a student devotes to the academic experience. The theory readily acknowledges that psychic and physical energy are finite and that educators are competing with other forces demanding a student's time and energy.

Astin's involvement theory has five postulates:

1. *Involvement refers to the investment of physical and psychological energy in various objects. The objects may be highly generalized (the student experience) or highly specific (preparing for a chemistry exam).*
2. *Regardless of its object, involvement occurs along a continuum; that is, different students manifest different degrees of involvement in different objects at different times.*
3. *Involvement has both quantitative and qualitative features. The extent of a student's involvement in academic work, for instance, can be measured quantitatively (how many hours the student spends studying) and qualitatively (whether the student reviews and comprehends reading assignments or simply stares at the textbook and daydreams).*
4. *The amount of student learning and personal development associated with any educational program is directly proportional to the quality and quantity of student involvement in that program.*
5. *The effectiveness of any educational policy or practice is directly related to the capacity of that policy or practice to increase student involvement* (1984b, p. 298).

The simplicity of the theory makes it attractive to both researchers and practitioners. A theory based on involvement has important implications for the style and form of teaching as well as for the programs and services of student affairs. Moreover, attention to students' involvement "provides a unifying construct that can help to focus the energies of all institutional personnel on a common objective" (Astin 1984b, p. 305). Supported by the recent report on the quality of higher education (Study Group 1984), this theory suggests a promising new student development theory for student affairs professionals performing as integrators within the institution.

Summary
Student development concepts and theories have been important to the direction of the student affairs profession for some time, but as a new role for student affairs emerges, several issues in student development must be addressed. First, studies reveal that practitioners do not generally understand or apply theories of student development. The use of student development theories is important to student affairs integrators who seek justification for programs and services, however, and who need the professional credibility necessary for a more central institutional role. Second, with increasing numbers of nontraditional students, theories and concepts in student development must be expanded to address differences in age, sex, and culture if student affairs professionals are to be able to develop programs and services that address those different needs and have the goal of social integration. Third, to promote student development and to achieve a greater integration of student and system needs, student and academic life, then the integration of student and organizational development must be attempted. Fourth, a new developmental theory—that of student involvement—may integrate other theories and provide a theoretical basis for the profession that complements current educational goals.

While student development theory faces a number of challenges, it remains important to the profession as an integrating concept for the role of the student affairs professional. The ability of the profession to redefine and apply its developmental orientation in a number of contexts and clienteles will in large part determine its future.

CONCLUSIONS AND RECOMMENDATIONS

The world of higher education is rarely static, and that statement is particularly true today. As a result of the wide array of changes and in response to them, the role of student affairs is evolving to one that is more central and critical to the achievement of other institutional goals, to one that seeks a greater integration of efforts by all within the institution, to one that is concerned about organizational development as a necessary complement to student development. Integrating many different needs and goals in the delivery of services calls on student affairs professionals to develop a wider range of skills, to exert leadership in new contexts, and to think of themselves in new ways. The new role that has been suggested—that of integrator—is in many ways not a new role, but an extension and realization of previous roles and a recognition of new student affairs efforts in a variety of areas.

A new role for student affairs demands responses by the profession. Similarly, a new role calls for responses by professional associations, by graduate programs preparing student affairs professionals, and by institutions seeking maximum effectiveness and vitality. The individual professional should not be alone in arguing his or her case for an expanded voice; growing recognition of this new role must be offered by graduate programs, by institutions, and by professional associations.

From this new role and from the example of recent student affairs efforts, a number of recommendations emerge. First, student affairs professionals must be prepared to take several steps:

Student affairs leaders must be able to understand the important isssues within their institution and be prepared to interpret their implications for student affairs.

1. *Assess the institutional environment.* Student affairs professionals must scan the environment to identify and interpret trends and events that have implications for their institution and the student affairs function. These trends include, but are not limited to, demographic changes, societal changes, economic trends, and politics surrounding the institution. Student affairs leaders, in the 1980s and beyond, can no longer afford to be isolationists.
2. *Comprehend institutional issues.* Student affairs leaders must be able to understand the important issues within their institution and be prepared to interpret their implications for student affairs, to suggest ways

in which student affairs can take leadership, and to alert others to important issues the institution must address. Perhaps more important, student affairs professionals must be able to assess and navigate the political waters surrounding often controversial institutional issues. To do so calls for enhanced analytic and political skills.

3. *Develop professional credibility with faculty.* To gain credibility with faculty, student affairs professionals must contribute in meaningful and significant ways to the academic experience, which must be articulated to faculty. Involvement in this area can be accomplished through more extensive research and evaluation, the presentation of findings through seminars, publications, and local and national professional activities, and teaching. Perhaps more important, student affairs can define for itself a role in academic quality. Student affairs leaders should capitalize on student involvement as a professional opportunity to build relationships with faculty.

4. *Become experts on students, their expectations, needs, interests, and abilities.* Despite being ''student experts'' in the institution, student affairs professionals often make little attempt to share their expertise with others. They must, however, more actively articulate that expertise to others in the institution in terms they find meaningful. But to be truly viewed as experts, the often anecdotal understanding of student affairs professionals must become grounded in systematic studies, assessments, and evaluations.

5. *Translate student affairs goals to others in the institution in meaningful terms.* While institutions tend to share a culture, different divisions within even the smallest of institutions share different personal and professional values. It is essential to understand those underlying values and to be able to translate student affairs goals in terms that are meaningful to others who possess a different set of values. To financial officers, for example, efforts designed to improve retention might be explained in terms of financial benefits to the institution; similarly, those efforts should be explained to faculty in terms of academic achievement.

6. *Contribute to the quality of the academic experience.* Just as student affairs has served other overriding needs within institutions, now is the time for it to also serve the goals of quality and the enhancement of the academic experience, which will come as a result of such efforts as intellectual theme programming and interest houses, counseling and advising, and participation in academic programs.

7. *Contribute to the effective and efficient management of institutions.* Student affairs leaders must understand and manage their organizations effectively to contribute to the overall managerial effectiveness of the institution, implying effective management of human and financial resources, program administration and evaluation, and planning. To do so will require more information than most student affairs divisions typically possess about students, costs, program effectiveness, and the like and so will require considerable effort to develop them.

8. *Develop appropriate skills.* Student affairs professionals, to meet the challenges of a new role, must avail themselves of opportunities to develop new skills—credit and noncredit courses and programs, campus-based programs, and programs and activities of national associations or higher education management institutes.

To accomplish these goals, student affairs professionals must be supported by their institutions. Therefore, institutions should seek to:

1. *Recognize, enhance, and support the efforts of student affairs.* Effective student affairs programs are essential to institutional survival and vitality (Baldridge, Kemerer, and Green 1982), and student affairs has a substantial role in the pursuit of academic quality and the retention of students (Study Group 1984). This evidence should be brought to the attention of institutional leaders as they seek to creatively address present and future challenges.

2. *Consider student affairs full partners in the institution.* Along with a recognition of the real and potential accomplishments of student affairs must come a

recognition that a stronger role for student affairs in the institution will contribute to institutional vitality and effectiveness in new ways. Student affairs professionals *can* take leadership in areas beyond their typical roles.

3. *Challenge student affairs professionals to make greater contributions.* Institutional leaders should expect student affairs staff to become more than disciplinarians, custodians, and educators; they should expect them to integrate students' and the institution's needs and to contribute meaningfully to institutional vitality. Institutional leaders should challenge them to develop the outlook, skills, and vision to look beyond their present roles.

To fulfill an expanded role, student affairs professionals need to develop a wider array of skills, and building skills must begin in the preparation of professionals. Therefore, graduate programs must:

1. *Develop present and future skills for the profession.* To be an effective student affairs professional takes more than counseling and human relations skills; it calls for management and planning skills, research and evaluation skills, political skills, the ability to understand and interpret organizations, and sensitivity to the many environments of higher education. Student affairs professionals are now engaged in a wider range of activities than ever before, and they will continue to broaden their activities in the future. These new activities demand a wider range of skills than most graduate preparation programs attempt to address, and they must be included at all levels of graduate preparation.

And, finally, the general national associations for student affairs professionals, the National Association of Student Personnel Administrators (NASPA), the American College Personnel Association (ACPA), and the National Association of Women Deans, Administrators, and Counselors (NAWDAC), should continue to provide leadership for the profession as it evolves to meet new roles. Specifically, the national associations must:

1. *Provide direction for the profession.* The national associations should define and emphasize the changing role of student affairs and recognize those efforts where student affairs staff are contributing in significant ways to the development of the profession and the vitality of the institution.
2. *Promote continuing professional education at all levels.* If student affairs is to meet the challenges of the present and the future, it must promote professional development to a greater extent than before. Skills appropriate to a new role and strategies to capitalize on new opportunities must be developed. Activities should be promoted at the individual, institutional, state, regional, and national levels. National associations for student affairs professionals must take leadership in designing efforts to meet the continuing professional development needs of a profession in transition.

If all components join forces, a new future for the profession can be realized, one with meaningful benefits to students, institutions, the student affairs profession, and the future of higher education. To do so will require significant efforts, particularly on the part of student affairs professionals, but while the efforts may be great, so too will be the benefits.

REFERENCES

The ERIC Clearinghouse on Higher Education abstracts and indexes the current literature on higher education for the National Institute of Education's monthly bibliographic journal, *Resources in Education*. Most of these publications are available through the ERIC Document Reproduction Service (EDRS). For publications cited in this bibliography that are available from EDRS, ordering number and price are included. Readers who wish to order a publication should write to the ERIC Document Reproduction Service, 3900 Wheeler Avenue, Alexandria, Virginia 22304. When ordering, please specify the document number. Documents are available as noted in microfiche (MF) and paper copy (PC). Because prices are subject to change, it is advisable to check the latest issue of *Resources in Education* for current cost based on the number of pages in the publication.

Abel, Janice. May 1978. "Gaining Power and Influence in the University: A Viewpoint." *Journal of College Student Personnel* 19: 238–41.

Abrams, Marjorie. Summer 1981. "Preparing Men and Women Students to Work Together: A New Student Development Challenge." *Journal of NAWDAC* 41: 3–8.

Aery, Shaila, and Moore, Norman. 1976. "Affecting Change in Student Services." Paper presented at the annual convention of the American Personnel and Guidance Association, March, Dallas, Texas. ED 128 693. 15 pp. MF–$0.97; PC–$3.54.

Aiken, James. Winter 1982. "Shifting Priorities: College Counseling Centers in the Eighties." *NASPA Journal* 19: 15–22.

American Council on Education. 1938. *The Student Personnel Point of View: A Report of a Conference*. Washington, D.C.: ACE.

Arner, T. D.; Peterson, W. D.; Arner, C. A.; Hawkins, L. T.; and Spooner, S. E. 1977. "Student Personnel Education: A Process-Outcome Model." *Journal of College Student Personnel* 17: 334–41.

Astin, Alexander W. 1975. *Preventing Students from Dropping Out*. San Francisco: Jossey-Bass.

———. Winter 1984a. "A Look at Pluralism in the Contemporary Student Population." *NASPA Journal* 21: 2–11.

———. July 1984b. "Student Involvement: A Developmental Theory for Higher Education." *Journal of College Student Personnel* 24: 297–308.

Astin, Alexander W., and others. 1984. *The American Freshman: National Norms for Fall 1983*. Los Angeles: University of California, Cooperative Institutional Research Program.

Balderston, Frederick E. 1978. *Managing Today's University.* San Francisco: Jossey-Bass.

Baldridge, J. Victor; Kemerer, Frank R.; and Green, Kenneth C. 1982. *The Enrollment Crisis: Factors, Actors, and Impacts.* AAHE-ERIC Higher Education Research Report No. 3. Washington, D.C.: American Association for Higher Education.

Baldridge, J. Victor, and Tierney, Michael. 1979. *New Approaches to Management.* San Francisco: Jossey-Bass.

Barnes, Stephen F.; Morton, W. Edward; and Austin, Alvin O. Spring 1984. "The Call for Accountability: The Struggle for Program Definition in Student Affairs." *NASPA Journal* 20: 10–20.

Beal, Philip E., and Noel, Lee. 1980. *What Works in Student Retention.* Boulder, Colo.: National Center for Higher Education Management Systems and the American College Testing Program.

Bender, Louis W. 1974. "Planning after the Golden Age." In *Improving Statewide Planning,* edited by James L. Wattenbarger and Louis Bender. New Directions for Higher Education No. 8. San Francisco: Jossey-Bass.

———. 1977. *Federal Regulation and Higher Education.* AAHE-ERIC Higher Education Research Report No. 1. Washington, D.C.: American Association for Higher Education.

Benezet, Louis T. 1979. "Future College Students and the Role of Student Affairs." In *The Student Affairs Dean and the President: Trends in Higher Education,* edited by David C. Tilley and others. Ann Arbor, Mich.: ERIC Clearinghouse on Counseling and Personnel Services. ED 169 459. 90 pp. MF–$0.97; PC not available EDRS.

Bennett, William J. 1984. *To Reclaim a Legacy: A Report on the Humanities in Higher Education.* Washington, D.C.: National Endowment for the Humanities.

Berdahl, Robert O. 1971. *Statewide Coordination of Higher Education.* Washington, D.C.: American Council on Education.

Biggs, D. A., and Skinner, K. A. May 1979. "A Decision-making Approach to Planning in Student Personnel." *Journal of College Student Personnel* 20: 258–64.

Blocker, C. E.; Bender, L.; and Martorana, S. V. 1975. *The Political Terrain: American Postsecondary Education.* Fort Lauderdale: Nova University Press.

Bloland, P. Summer 1979. "Student Personnel Training for the Chief Student Affairs Officer: Essential or Unnecessary?" *NASPA Journal* 17: 57–62.

Bok, Derek C. 1976. "Can Ethics Be Taught?" *Change* 8: 8+.

Borland, David T. 1980. "Organizational Development: A Professional Imperative." In *Student Development in Higher Education,* edited by Don G. Creamer. Cincinnati: American College Personnel Association.

Borland, David T., and Thomas, R. E. March 1976. "Student Development Implementation through Expanded Professional Skills." *Journal of College Student Personnel* 17: 145–49.

Boulding, Kenneth E. 1975. "The Management of Decline." *Change* 7: 5+.

Brodzinski, Frederick R. 1978. "The Future of Student Services: Parameters, Resources, and Consumer Interests." Paper presented at the First National Conference on Student Services, October, Madison, Wisconsin. ED 175 327. 30 pp. MF–$0.97; PC–$5.34.

———. Summer 1979. "Campus 1999: A Scenario." *NASPA Journal* 17: 52–56.

Brown, R. D. 1972. *Student Development in Tomorrow's Higher Education: A Return to the Academy.* Student Personnel Series No. 16. Washington, D.C.: American College Personnel Association.

———. May 1985a. "Accountability and Student Development." *Journal of College Student Personnel* 26: 195–96.

———. Winter 1985b. "Graduate Education for the Student Development Educator: A Content and Process Model." *NASPA Journal* 22: 38–43.

Brown, Suzanne. Spring 1981. "An Evaluation Process for Student Affairs Agencies." *NASPA Journal* 18: 2–13.

Brubacher, John S. 1971. *The Courts and Higher Education.* Rutherford, N.J.: Fairleigh Dickinson University Press.

Brubacher, John S., and Rudy, W. 1976. *Higher Education in Transition.* New York: Harper & Row.

Canon, Harry J. 1980. "Developing Staff Potential." In *Student Services,* edited by U. Delworth and G. Hanson. San Francisco: Jossey-Bass.

———. March 1984. "Developmental Tasks for the Profession: The Next 25 Years." *Journal of College Student Personnel* 25: 105–11.

Carnegie Commission on Higher Education. 1971. *The Capitol and the Campus.* New York: McGraw-Hill.

Carnegie Council on Policy Studies in Higher Education. 1975. *More Than Survival: Prospects for Higher Education in a Period of Uncertainty.* San Francisco: Jossey-Bass.

———. 1980. *Three Thousand Futures.* San Francisco: Jossey-Bass.

Carpenter, D. Stanley, and Miller, Theodore K. Summer 1981. "An Analysis of Professional Development in Student Affairs Work." *NASPA Journal* 19: 2–11.

Casper, Irene G., and Morey, Ruth A. 1976. "Management Information Systems and the Role of Student Affairs." Paper presented at the annual convention of the National Association of Student Personnel Administrators, April, Chicago, Illinois. ED 138 909. 19 pp. MF–$0.97; PC not available EDRS.

Centra, John A. 1980. "College Enrollments in the 1980s: Projections and Possibilities." *Journal of Higher Education* 51: 19–38.

Cheit, Earl F. 1971. *The New Depression in Higher Education.* New York: McGraw-Hill.

Chickering, Arthur W. 1969. *Education and Identity.* San Francisco: Jossey-Bass.

———. 1974. *Commuting versus Resident Students: Overcoming Educational Inequities of Living Off Campus.* San Francisco: Jossey-Bass.

Chickering, Arthur W., and associates. 1981. *The Modern American College: Responding to the New Realities of Diverse Students and a Changing Society.* San Francisco: Jossey-Bass.

College Entrance Examination Board. 1980. *Undergraduate Admissions: The Realities of Institutional Policies, Practices, and Procedures.* New York: CEEB. ED 196 351. 86 pp. MF–$0.97; PC not available EDRS.

Cope, Robert G. 1981. *Strategic Planning, Management, and Decision Making.* AAHE-ERIC Higher Education Research Report No. 9. Washington, D.C.: American Association for Higher Education.

Council of Student Personnel Associations. November 1975. "Student Development Services in Postsecondary Education." *Journal of College Student Personnel* 16: 524–28.

Cowley, W. H. 1949. "Some History and a Venture in Prophecy." In *Trends in Student Personnel Work,* edited by E. G. Williamson. Minneapolis: University of Minnesota Press.

Cox, David W., and Ivy, William A. Summer 1984. "Staff Development Needs of Student Affairs Professionals." *NASPA Journal* 22: 26–33.

Creamer, Don G., ed. 1980. *Student Development in Higher Education: Theories, Practices, and Future Directions.* Washington, D.C.: American College Personnel Association.

Cross, K. Patricia. 1981a. *Adults as Learners.* San Francisco: Jossey-Bass.

———. March 1981b. "Planning for the Future of the Student Personnel Profession." *Journal of College Student Personnel* 22: 99–104.

Davis, James R. Summer 1980. "Students in the 1980s: Get Ready for the Calculating Consumers." *NASPA Journal* 18: 15–20.

DeCoster, David A., and Mable, Phyllis, eds. 1981. *Understanding Today's Students*. New Directions for Student Services No. 16. San Francisco: Jossey-Bass.

Deegan, William L. 1981. *Managing Student Affairs Programs: Methods, Models, and Muddles*. Palm Springs, Calif.: ETC Publications.

Delworth, Ursala; Hanson, Gary; and associates. 1980. *Student Services: A Handbook for the Profession*. San Francisco: Jossey-Bass.

Demetrulias, Diana A. M.; Sattler, Joan L.; and Graham, Leslie P. Summer 1982. "How Do You Know When You Are Hungry?: Disabled Students in University Settings." *Journal of NAWDAC* 45: 8–13.

Desruisseaux, Paul. July 1985. "Gifts to Higher Education Reach Record $5.6 Billion; Businesses, Foundations, Individuals All Increase Aid." *Chronicle of Higher Education* 30: 1 + .

Dewey, Mary Evelyn. Winter 1972. "The Student Personnel Worker of 1980." *Journal of NAWDAC* 35: 59–64.

Edwards, H. T., and Nordin, V. D. 1979. *Higher Education and the Law*. Cambridge: Harvard University, Institute for Educational Management.

Erikson, Erik. 1963. *Identity: Youth and Crisis*. New York: W. W. Norton.

Erwin, T. Daryl, and Miller, Stephen. Spring 1985. "Technology and the Three R's." *NASPA Journal* 22: 47–51.

Eulau, Heinz, and Quinley, Harold. 1970. *State Officials and Higher Education*. New York: McGraw-Hill.

Fenske, Robert H. 1980. "Historical Foundations." In *Student Services: A Handbook for the Profession,* edited by Ursala Delworth, Gary Hanson, and associates. San Francisco: Jossey-Bass.

"Foreign Students in U.S. Institutions, 1983–84." 5 September 1984. *Chronicle of Higher Education* 29: 21.

Foxley, Cecelia H., ed. 1980a. *Applying Management Techniques*. New Directions for Student Services No. 9. San Francisco: Jossey-Bass.

————. 1980b. "Determinants of Managerial Effectiveness." In *Applying Management Techniques,* edited by Cecelia H. Foxley. New Directions for Student Services No. 9. San Francisco: Jossey-Bass.

Friedan, Betty. 1981. *The Second Stage*. New York: Summit Books.

Geller, William W. July 1982. "Strengthening the Academic–Student Affairs Relationship." *Journal of College Student Personnel* 23: 355–57.

Glenny, Lyman A. July/August 1980. "Demographic and Related Issues for Higher Education in the 1980s." *Journal of Higher Education* 51: 363–80.

Gouldner, H. May/June 1980. "The Social Implications of Campus Litigation." *Journal of Higher Education* 51: 328–36.

Grabowski, Stanley M. 1981. *Marketing in Higher Education.* AAHE-ERIC Higher Education Research Report No. 5. Washington, D.C.: American Association for Higher Education.

Green, Kenneth C. April 1983. "Retention: An Old Solution Finds a New Problem." *AAHE Bulletin* 35: 3–6.

Greenfeig, Beverly R., and Goldberg, Barbara J. March 1984. "Orienting Returning Adult Students." In *Orienting Students to College,* edited by M. Lee Upcraft. New Directions for Student Services No. 25. San Francisco: Jossey-Bass.

Hall, Charles W. L. May 1981. *Professional Development within the Division of Student Affairs.* Hattiesburg: University of Southern Mississippi. ED 226 300. 29 pp. MF–$0.97; PC not available EDRS.

Hameister, Brenda. March 1984. "Orienting Disabled Students." In *Orienting Students to College,* edited by M. Lee Upcraft. New Directions for Student Services No. 25. San Francisco: Jossey-Bass.

Harpel, Richard L. Winter 1975. "Accountability: Current Demands on Student Personnel Programs." *NASPA Journal* 12: 144–57.

———. Summer 1976. "Planning, Budgeting, and Evaluation in Student Affairs Programs: A Manual for Administrators." *NASPA Journal* 14: i–xx.

Harvey, Thomas R. March 1976. "Student Development and the Future of Higher Education: A Force Analysis." *Journal of College Student Personnel* 17: 90–94.

Heath, Douglas. 1968. *Growing Up in College: Liberal Education and Maturity.* San Francisco: Jossey-Bass.

Hencley, S. P., and Yates, J. R. eds. 1974. *Futurism in Education: Methodologies.* Berkeley, Calif.: McCutchan.

Hester, Susan B., and Dickerson, Kitty G. November 1982. "The Emerging Dual Career Lifestyle: Are Your Students Prepared for It?" *Journal of College Student Personnel* 23: 514–19.

Hodgkinson, Harold L. 1984. "Students in the 1980s: Demography and Values." Paper presented at the National Conference in Higher Education, American Association for Higher Education, March, Chicago, Illinois.

Hughes, Rees. Winter 1983. "The Nontraditional Student in Higher Education: A Synthesis of the Literature." *NASPA Journal* 20: 51–64.

Hurst, J. C. 1980. "Challenges for the Future." In *Dimensions of Intervention for Student Development,* edited by W. H. Morrill, J. C. Hurst, and E. R. Oettings. New York: John Wiley & Sons.

Iannaccone, L. 1967. *Politics in Education.* New York: Center for Applied Research in Education.

Johnson, Cynthia S. Spring 1984. "Special Technology." *NASPA Journal* 21: 17–23.

Johnson, Cynthia S., and Foxley, Cecelia H. 1980. "Devising Tools for Middle Managers." In *Student Services: A Handbook for the Profession,* edited by Ursala Delworth, Gary Hanson, and associates. San Francisco: Jossey-Bass.

Johnson, Cynthia S., and Pyle, Richard K., eds. 1984. *Enhancing Student Development with Computers.* New Directions for Student Services No. 26. San Francisco: Jossey-Bass.

Johnson, Debra Hazel, and Steele, Brenton H. May 1984. "A National Survey of Research Activity in Student Affairs Divisions." *Journal of College Student Personnel* 25: 200–205.

Jones, John D. Spring 1978. "Student Personnel Work: Current State and Future Directions." *NASPA Journal* 15: 2–11.

Jones, Landon Y. 1980. *Great Expectations.* New York: Coward, McCann, Geoghegan.

Kaplan, W. A. 1978. *The Law of Higher Education.* San Francisco: Jossey-Bass.

Kasworm, C. E. March 1980. "Student Services for the Older Undergraduate Student." *Journal of College Student Personnel* 21: 163–69.

Keller, George C. 1983. *Academic Strategy: The Management Revolution in American Higher Education.* Baltimore: Johns Hopkins University Press.

Kerr, Clark. 1971. *The Uses of the University.* Cambridge: Harvard University Press.

Kinnick, Bernard C., and Bolheimer, R. L. Fall 1984. "College Presidents' Perceptions of Student Affairs Issues and Development Needs of Chief Student Affairs Officers." *NASPA Journal* 22: 2–9.

Knefelkamp, Lee L. 1978. *Applying New Developmental Findings.* New Directions for Student Services No. 4. San Francisco: Jossey-Bass.

Knock, G. H., ed. 1977. *Perspectives on the Preparation of Student Affairs Professionals.* Student Personnel Series No. 22. Washington, D.C.: American College Personnel Association.

Kohlberg, L. 1969. "Stage and Sequence in the Cognitive Developmental Approach to Socialization." In *Handbook of Socialization Theory and Research,* edited by D. Goslin. Chicago: Rand-McNally.

Kramer, Martin M. 1980. *The Venture Capital of Higher Education.* Berkeley, Calif.: Carnegie Council on Policy Studies in Higher Education.

Kuh, George D. Spring 1981. "Beyond Student Development: Contemporary Priorities for Student Affairs." *NASPA Journal* 18: 29–36.

———, ed. 1983. *Understanding Student Affairs Organizations.* New Directions for Student Services No. 23. San Francisco: Jossey-Bass.

———. January 1984. "A Framework for Understanding Student Affairs Organizations." *Journal of College Student Personnel* 25: 25–31.

Kuh, George D.; Donnells, M.; Doherty, P.; and Gamshaw, P. F. 1977. "Student Development Theory in Practice." *NASPA Journal* 16: 48–52.

Lamont, Lansing. 1979. *Campus Shock.* New York: E. P. Dutton.

Lasch, Christopher. 1978. *Culture of Narcissism.* New York: W. W. Norton & Co.

Lenning, Oscar T.; Beal, Philip E.; and Sauer, Ken. 1980. *Retention and Attrition: Evidence for Actions and Research.* Boulder, Colo.: NCHEMS.

Lenning, Oscar T.; Sauer, Ken; and Beal, Philip E. 1980. *Student Retention Strategies.* AAHE-ERIC Higher Education Research Report No. 8. Washington, D.C.: American Association for Higher Education.

Leslie, Larry L. January/February 1980. "The Financial Prospects for Higher Education in the 1980s." *Journal of Higher Education* 15: 1–17.

Leslie, Larry L., and Miller, H. F., Jr. 1974. *Higher Education and the Steady State.* AAHE-ERIC Higher Education Research Report No. 4. Washington, D.C.: American Association for Higher Education.

Levine, Arthur. 1980. *When Dreams and Heroes Died.* San Francisco: Jossey-Bass.

Levinson, Daniel, and others. 1978. *The Seasons of a Man's Life.* New York: Ballantine.

Lewis, C. T.; Leach, E. R.; and Lutz, L. L. 1983. "A Marketing Model for Student Retention." *NASPA Journal* 20: 15–19.

Litten, Larry. January/February 1980. "Marketing Higher Education." *Journal of Higher Education* 51: 40–59.

McBee, Mary Luise. Summer 1982. "Helping Handicapped Students Succeed in College." *Journal of NAWDAC* 45: 3–7.

McConnell, T. R. July 1970. "Student Personnel Services: Central or Peripheral?" *NASPA Journal* 8: 55–63.

Martorana, S. V., and Corbett, Patricia C. 1983. *State Legislation Affecting Community, Junior, and Two-Year Technical Colleges, 1982*. University Park, Pa.: Pennsylvania State University, Center for the Study of Higher Education.

Matthews, Jana B., and Norgaard, Rolf. 1984. *Managing the Partnership between Higher Education and Industry*. Boulder, Colo.: NCHEMS.

Meabon, David L.; Suddick, David E.; Owens, Hilda F.; and Klein, Anna C. Spring 1981. "A Reexamination of the National Trends of Management Techniques in Student Affairs." *Journal of College Student Personnel* 18: 14–21.

Mendenhall, W. R.; Miller, T. K.; and Winston, R. B., eds. 1982. *Administration and Leadership in Student Affairs*. Muncie, Ind.: Accelerated Development.

Millard, R. M. 1976. *State Boards of Higher Education*. AAHE-ERIC Higher Education Research Report No. 4. Washington, D.C.: American Association for Higher Education.

Miller, T. K., and Prince, Judith 1977. *The Future of Student Affairs*. San Francisco: Jossey-Bass.

Mingle, James R., and Norris, Donald M. 1981. "Institutional Strategies for Responding to Decline." In *Challenges of Retrenchment*, by James R. Mingle and associates. San Francisco: Jossey-Bass.

Moos, Rudolph H. 1979. *Evaluating Educational Environments*. San Francisco: Jossey-Bass.

Morrill, W. H. 1980. "Training Student Affairs Professionals." In *Dimensions of Intervention for Student Development*, edited by W. H. Morrill, J. C. Hurst, and E. R. Oettings. New York: John Wiley & Sons.

Morrill, W. H., and Banning, J. 1973. "Dimensions of Training Campus Mental Health Professionals." Mimeographed. Boulder, Colo.: WICHE Task Force on Training.

Morrill, W. H.; Hurst, J. C.; and Oettings, E. R., eds. 1980. *Dimensions of Intervention for Student Development*. New York: John Wiley & Sons.

Mortimer, K. P., and Tierney, M. L. 1979. *The Three "R's" of the Eighties: Reduction, Retrenchment, and Reallocation*. AAHE-ERIC Higher Education Research Report No. 4. Washington, D.C.: American Association for Higher Education.

Mueller, Kate H. 1961. *Student Personnel Work in Higher Education*. Boston: Houghton-Mifflin.

Murphy, J. T. 1980. *The State Role in Education: Past Research and Future Directions*. Palo Alto, Calif.: Stanford University, Institute for Research on Educational Finance and Governance. ED 193 798. 36 pp. MF–$0.97; PC–$.

Meyers-Briggs, I. 1962. *Meyers-Briggs Type Indicator*. Princeton, N.J.: Educational Testing Service.

Naisbitt, John. 1982. *Megatrends*. New York: Warner Books.

National Commission on Excellence in Education. 1983. *A Nation at Risk*. Washington, D.C.: National Institute of Education.

Nelson, J., and Murphy, H. 1980. "The Projected Effects of Enrollment and Budget Reductions on Student Personnel Services." *NASPA Journal* 17: 2–10.

Newton, Fred B., and Richardson, Robert L. September 1976. "Expected Entry-level Competencies of Student Personnel Workers." *Journal of College Student Personnel* 17: 426–30.

O'Keefe, Michael. May/June 1985. "Whatever Happened to the Crash of '80, '81, '82, '83, '84, '85?" *Change* 17: 37–41.

Ostar, Allen W. 1 July 1985. "Quality and Equality in Higher Education." *Higher Education and National Affairs* 34: 7.

Ostroth, D. David. January 1981. "Competencies for Entry-level Professionals: What Do Employers Look for When Hiring New Staff?" *Journal of College Student Personnel* 22: 5–11.

Ostroth, D. David; Efird, Frances D.; and Lerman, Lewis S. September 1984. "Career Patterns of Chief Student Affairs Officers." *Journal of College Student Personnel* 25: 443–47.

Palm, Richard L. Fall 1984. "Student Personnel Administration at the Small College." *NASPA Journal* 22: 48–55.

Palmer, Stacy E. 11 July 1984. "Adult Enrollments." *Chronicle of Higher Education* 28: 13.

Papler, D. R. 1977. "Is There a Lawyer in the House?" *Change* 9: 14–16.

Parker, Dolores, and Eliason, Carol. July 1980. *Adult Counseling for Sex Equity in Postsecondary Education*. Washington, D.C.: Department of Health, Education, and Welfare, Office of Education, Women's Educational Equity Act Program. ED 192 176. 57 pp. MF–$0.97; PC–$7.14.

Perry, W., Jr. 1970. *Forms of Intellectual and Ethical Development in the College Years: A Scheme*. New York: Holt, Rinehart & Winston.

Pillinger, B. B., and Kraack, T. A. Winter 1981. "Long-range Planning: A Key to Effective Management." *NASPA Journal* 18: 8–17.

Pirnot, Karen A., and Dunn, Wendy L. Summer 1983. "Value Priorities of Adult Students." *Journal of NAWDAC* 46: 22–25.

Priest, Douglas M.; Alphenaar, W. J.; and Boer, W. J. Summer 1980. "Long-range Planning: Implications and Applications for the Chief Student Personnel Administrator." *NASPA Journal* 18: 2–7.

Pruitt, Anne S. March 1979. "Preparation of Student Development Specialists during the 1980s." *Counselor Education and Supervision* 18: 190–98.

Racippo, Vincent C., and Foxley, Cecelia H. 1980. "MIS: A Tool for Planning and Evaluation." In *Applying Management Techniques,* edited by Cecelia H. Foxley. New Directions for Student Services No. 9. San Francisco: Jossey-Bass.

Rhatigan, James J. Fall 1979. "Looking Forward to the 1980s." *NASPA Journal* 17: 2–10.

Rickard, S. January 1972. "The Role of the Chief Student Personnel Administrator Revisited." *NASPA Journal* 9: 219–26.

Rodgers, Robert F. 1982. "Using Theory in Practice." In *Administration and Leadership in Student Affairs,* edited by W. R. Mendenhall, T. K. Miller, and R. B. Winston. Muncie, Ind.: Accelerated Development.

Rosenthal, A., and Fuhrman, S. 1981. *Legislative Education Leadership in the States.* Washington, D.C.: Institute for Educational Leadership.

Rudolph, Frederick. 1962. *The American College and University.* New York: Vintage Books.

Rumberger, Russel W. July/August 1984. "The Job Market for College Graduates, 1960–90." *Journal of Higher Education* 55: 433–54.

Sampson, James P., Jr. Winter 1982. "Effective Computer Resource Management: Keeping the Tail from Wagging the Dog." *NASPA Journal* 19: 38–46.

Sandeen, Arthur. Fall 1982. "Professional Preparation Programs in Student Personnel Services in Higher Education: A National Assessment by Chief Student Affairs Officers." *NASPA Journal* 20: 51–58.

Sanford, Nevitt. 1962. *The American College.* New York: John Wiley & Sons.

Saurman, K., and Nash, R. 1975. "MBO, Student Development, and Accountability." *NASPA Journal* 13: 179–89.

Schroeder, R. G. 1975. "An Approach for Improved Planning in Colleges." Paper presented at Institute of Management Science and Operations Research Society of America, May, Chicago, Illinois.

Schumpeter, Joseph. 1934. *The Theory of Economic Development.* Cambridge: Harvard University Press.

Shaffer, R. H. 1973. "An Emerging Role of Student Personnel: Contributing to Organizational Effectiveness." *Journal of College Student Personnel* 14: 386–91.

————. March 1984. "Critical Dimensions of Student Affairs in the Decades Ahead." *Journal of College Student Personnel* 25: 112–14.

Shay, John E., Jr. Fall 1984. "Point of View: The Chief Student Affairs Officer and the President: Revisiting an Old Issue." *NASPA Journal* 22: 55–58.

Silverman, Robert J. January 1971. "The Student Personnel Worker on the Boundary." *Journal of College Student Personnel* 12: 3–6.

————. Fall 1980. "The Student Personnel Administrator as a Leading Edge Leader." *NASPA Journal* 18: 10–15.

Smith, Daryl G. Spring 1982. "The Next Step beyond Student Development: Becoming Partners within Our Institutions." *NASPA Journal* 19: 53–62.

Spooner, Susan E. January 1979. "Preparing the Student Development Specialist: The Process-Outcome Model Applied." *Journal of College Student Personnel* 20: 45–53.

Stadtman, Verne A. 1980. *Academic Adaptations: Higher Education Prepares for the 1980s and 1990s*. San Francisco: Jossey-Bass.

Stafford, Thomas H., Jr.; Marion, Paul B.; and Salter, M. Lee. Summer 1980. "Adjustment of International Students." *NASPA Journal* 18: 40–45.

Stamatakos, Louis C., and Rogers, Russell B. September 1984. "Student Affairs: A Profession in Need of a Philosophy." *Journal of College Student Personnel* 25: 400–411.

Stark, Joan S., and associates. 1977. *The Many Faces of Educational Consumerism*. Lexington, Mass.: Lexington Books.

Strange, C. 1981. "Organizational Barriers to Student Development." *NASPA Journal* 19: 12–20.

Strange, C., and Contomanolis, E. 1983. "Knowledge Perceptions of Human Development Theory among Student Affairs Masters Students." *Journal of College Student Personnel* 24: 197–201.

"Student Services Key in Retention Project." 25 June 1984. *National On-Campus Report* 25: 1.

Study Group on the Conditions of Excellence in American Higher Education. 1984. *Involvement in Learning: Realizing the Potential of American Higher Education*. Washington, D.C.: National Institute of Education.

Suchinsky, Richard T. Spring 1982. "Psychological Characteristics of the 1980s College Student: An Exploration of the Psychologic Processes Involved in the Development of the Narcissistic Character Pattern." *NASPA Journal* 19: 13–22.

Thomas, Russell E.; Murrell, Patricia; and Chickering, Arthur W. Summer 1982. "Critical Role of Value Development in Student Development." *NASPA Journal* 20: 3–13.

Toffler, Alvin. 1970. *Future Shock.* New York: Bantam Books.

Truitt, J. W., and Gross, R. F. 1970. "In-Service Education for College Student Personnel." In *New Dimensions in Student Personnel Administration,* edited by O. R. Herron, Jr. Scranton, Pa.: International Textbook Co.

University of Minnesota. 1981. "Planning and Evaluation Information in the Office of Student Affairs: Review and Recommendations." *Office of Student Affairs Research Bulletin* 22 (3). Minneapolis: Author. ED 214 473. 96 pp. MF–$0.97; PC–$9.36.

Upcraft, M. L.; Finney, J. E.; and Garland, Peter. 1984. "Orientation: A Context." In *Orienting Students to College,* edited by M. Lee Upcraft. New Directions for Student Services No. 25. San Francisco: Jossey-Bass.

Upcraft, M. L.; Peterson, P. C.; and Moore, B. L. 1981. *The Academic and Personal Development of Penn State Freshmen.* University Park, Pa.: Pennsylvania State University.

Vasquez, M. J., and Chavez, E. L. 1980. "Unique Student Populations." In *Dimensions of Intervention for Student Development,* edited by W. H. Morrill, J. C. Hurst, and E. R. Oettings. New York: John Wiley & Sons.

Weathersby, R. P., and Tarule, J. M. 1980. *Adult Development: Implications for Higher Education.* AAHE-ERIC Higher Education Research Report No. 4. Washington, D.C.: American Association for Higher Education.

Wheaton, Janilee B., and Robinson, Daniel C. Fall 1983. "Responding to the Needs of Reentry Women: A Comprehensive Campus Model." *NASPA Journal* 21: 44–51.

Widick, Carole; Knefelkamp, Lee; and Parker, Clyde A. 1980. "Student Development." In *Student Services: A Handbook for the Profession,* edited by Ursala Delworth, Gary Hanson, and associates. San Francisco: Jossey-Bass.

Williamson, E. G., ed. 1949. *Trends in Student Personnel Work.* Minneapolis: University of Minnesota Press.

Wright, Doris J. 1984. "Orienting Minority Students." In *Orienting Students to College,* edited by M. Lee Upcraft. New Directions for Student Services No. 25. San Francisco: Jossey-Bass.

INDEX

A

Ability vs. aspiration, 33
Academic advising
    adult student needs, 35
    faculty/student affairs role, 66
    growth of, 5
    need for, 46, 63, 84
    role in retention, 48–49, 64, 83
Academic affairs, 56
Academic deference from courts, 23
Academic dishonesty, 38
Academic probation: counseling, 50
Academic support function, 7, 13, 65
Academically underprepared, 11, 33, 36, 48, 85
Access to education, 11, 30–31, 33
Access to learning services, 35
Accountability
    funds, 25
    higher education, 1, 14, 21–23
    information processing model, 75
    student affairs programs, 55
ACPA (see American College Personnel Association)
ACT score decline, 33
ADAM (Acquisition of Data for Accountability and Management)
  model, 75
Adjustment
    cultural: foreign students, 31–32
    disabled students, 34
Administrative skills, 91–93
Admissions (see also Preadmission), 6, 23, 64, 67
Adult development 101–102
Adult students, 11, 30, 34–35, 101
Affirmative action, 23
Aging society, 14
Agricultural majors, 37
Alumni
    activities, 52
    career networks, 85
    support, 69
American Council on Education, 5
American College Personnel Association (ACPA), 6, 110
Architectural barriers, 34
Army: use of testing/counseling, 5
Aspiration vs. ability, 33
Assertiveness training, 30
Athletics, 4, 5

Attrition rates/costs (see also Retention), 31, 48
Azusa Pacific University: student retention, 2

B
Baby boom, 1, 11, 13–14
Bachelor's as terminal degree, 37
Basic skills, 33, 84
Behavior codes, 40
Biggs and Skinner planning model, 76
Birth rate, 1, 11–12
Black students, 11, 30
Bryn Mawr College: summer program for women, 97
Budget reductions, 26
Budgeting skills, 77–78
Business majors, 36, 37
Business/industry relationships, 21, 53–54

C
California: retention efforts, 2, 7
Career choice, 36–37
Career planning, 5, 13, 15, 35, 38, 40, 48, 63, 66, 85
Career planning networks, 54, 85
Career pressures, 14
Carson-Newman College: Project RETAIN, 50
Change rate, 18
Chapman College: student retention, 2
Cheating, 38
Civil rights, 23, 24
Cocurricular interest houses, 67
Collaboration
        business and colleges, 53–54
        faculty and student affairs workers, 66–67
College attendance: recognition of benefits, 30
College choice, 63
Community College of Allegheny County:
        student activities management system, 44, 85
Commuter students, 27, 46, 84
Competencies: entry level student affairs, 93–94
Competition
        funds, 14, 21, 79
        jobs, 13
        students, 21, 46, 63
Compliance with state/federal statutes, 22, 23
Computer-assisted systems, 44, 45, 77, 85
Computer science majors, 37
Constitutional rights, 23, 24

Consumer orientation
    student affairs, 67–70
    student attitudes, 24, 38–39
Continuing professional education, 72, 95–98, 111
Contractual obligations, 24, 25, 39
Cooperative education, 54
Cooperative Institutional Research Project, 37
Cost information needs, 22
Council for Financial Aid to Education, 51
Counseling
    development of, 5, 6
    need for, 13, 30, 35, 40, 63, 84
    role in retention, 48, 50, 64, 83
Court litigation, 23–25, 39, 51
Credibility: student affairs, 67, 71, 82, 91, 101, 103, 108
Cultural activity funds, 53
Cultural differences, 31–32, 101
Curriculum development
    student, 65
    student personnel professionals, 89–91
Custodian role, 4–5

D

Day care services, 30
Dean of personnel: first, 4
Debating societies, 4
Decision-making: student affairs, 44
Degrees: expansion of, 41
Demographic changes, 11–14, 70
Development activities, 52
Developmental theory (see Student development)
Disabled, 11, 33–34, 36, 84, 91
Disciplinarian role, 3–4
Discipline of students, 4, 23, 40
Discretionary funds, 26
Discrimination, 24, 30
Dishonesty, 38
Doctoral programs: student personnel, 92
Dropout prevention, 46, 50, 65
Due process, 23, 24, 39

E

"Early warning system": retention, 46, 65
Education policy, 21–23
Education-work relationship, 18
Educator role, 5–7

Eliot, Charles William, 4
Endowment funds, 53
Engineering majors, 35, 57
English proficiency, 32
Enrollment management, 45–47, 50, 66, 84
Enrollment projections, 12
Equal opportunity, 23, 33
Evaluation skills, 80–81
Evaluations: formal, 74
Exit interviews, 65
Extracurricular activities
    development of, 4, 27
    narcissistic attitude, 18, 38, 40
    relationship to retention, 65

F

Faculty development, 65
Faculty relationships, 58, 62, 66, 108
Family counseling, 30
Family influence, 31, 32, 35
Federal accountability, 23
Federal aid (see Student financial aid)
Federal regulations, 23
Financial conditions, 25–26
Financial aid (see Private financial support; Student financial aid)
Financial management skills, 77–78, 85
Financial problems, 32, 75, 103
Fine arts majors, 37
Food services, 6
Foreign students, 31–32, 35
Forestry majors, 37
Fraternities, 4
Frostburg State College: information processing, 75
Fund-raising, 42, 52
Furman University
    student affairs planning, 44
    SWOTS program assessment, 75

G

Generalists: need for, 18
Global issues, 19
Goal integration, 62–66, 108
Goal-setting
    institutional, 74
    student affairs, 44, 78
Grade tracking, 45

Graduate programs: student personnel, 89–96, 98, 110
Greek letter societies, 4, 86

H

Handbooks: management strategies, 54
Handicapped (see Disabled)
Harvard University
      first personnel dean, 4
      Institute for Educational Management, 97
Harvey Mudd College: student retention, 2
Health and fitness focus, 18
Health services, 5
High school completion rate: Hispanics, 30
High school preparation, 33
High school students: research on, 80
Higher education
      as a state agency, 22
      changes, 1–2, 41–43
      "golden age," 25
      "new depression," 25
      political trends, 21–27
Hispanic students, 11, 12, 30
History of student affairs, 1–7
Homesickness, 32
Housing, 6, 32, 65, 83
Human development theory, 101–102
Human relations skills, 92–93
Human resource management, 78
Humanities majors, 37

I

In loco parentis, 3, 6, 24, 39
Independent study, 32
Industrial change, 14–15
Information age, 1, 14–16, 36
Information sources, 77
Information systems, 44–45, 75–77
Inservice education, 95
Institute for Educational Management, 97
Institutional image, 46, 48, 63
"Institutional integrator" role, 3, 7, 47, 57–72, 103
Institutional mission, 19, 46, 81, 102
Institutional relationship, 2, 40, 48, 56–58, 62–66, 81–82, 97,
    107–110
Institutional researchers, 67
Institutional vitality, 41–42

Instructional techniques, 41
International students, 31–32, 35
Internships, 54, 85
Interpreters for disabled, 34
Interviewing center, 54
Involvement in Learning, 26

J

Job descriptions, 74
John Jay College of Criminal Justice: retention strategy, 50
Judicial influence, 23

L

Law majors, 36
Leadership role, 58, 62
Learning disabilities (see Disabled)
Learning skills centers, 33
Learning styles, 12, 30
Legal issues, 23–25, 50–51
Legislation increases, 22, 23
Liability, 25, 51
Liberal arts career internships, 85
Life goals, 37
Life stages, 102
Lifelong learning, 15, 19
Lifestyle counseling, 30
Literary societies, 4
Litigation (see Court litigation)
Long-range planning, 43, 76, 87
Longitudinal studies, 80
Loyola Marymount University: student retention, 2

M

Mainstreaming student affairs, 60–62
Majors, 37
Management information systems, 76–77
Management skills, 73–78, 91–93, 97
Management strategies, 54
Management system: student activities, 44
Marketing, 46–47, 63–64
Math skills, 33
"Me-ism," 17
Miami-Dade Community College: grade tracking, 45
Middle-aged society, 13
Minority students, 1, 12–13, 30–31, 35, 84, 91, 97
Mission statements, 46, 74

Models
    accountability, 55
    ADAM information processing, 75
    Biggs and Skinner planning, 76
    POWS planning/evaluation, 75
    resource management, 23
    Schroeder planning, 76
    Student Affairs Program Evaluation Process, 75
    student development, 6
    student personnel curriculum, 90, 94–96
    SWOTS program assessment, 75
Monitoring student progress, 85
Montana State University: career planning, 85
Mount St. Mary's College: student retention, 2

N
Narcissism, 17–18, 38, 39
National Association of Student Personnel Administrators
    (NASPA), 55, 110
National Association of Women Deans, Administrators, and
    Counselors (NAWDAC), 110
National Center for Higher Education Management Systems, 23
National surveys: retention strategies, 49
Native Americans, 30–31
NAWDAC (see National Association of Women Deans,
    Administrators, and Counselors)
Networks: career placement, 54, 85
Nontraditional careers, 16, 37
Nontraditional students, 11, 29–36, 42, 69, 84–85
North Carolina State University: foreign students, 32
"Now" generation, 17

O
Older students, 30, 34–35
Opportunity as a profession, 60–62
Organizational change, 103
Organizational skills, 81–82, 89, 93, 97
Orientation, 6, 34, 65, 67, 83, 84
Outcome information needs, 22
Outreach programs, 48

P
Parents association, 7, 52
Part-time students, 27, 32–33, 36, 84

Pennsylvania State University
>funds for interviewing center, 54
>parents association, 7, 52
Performing arts majors, 37
Persister characteristics, 64
Personal success motivation, 37–38
Physical disabilities (see Disabled)
Pitzer College: student retention, 2
Plagiarism, 38
Planning
>commissions, 22
>comprehensive, 43–44
>need for, 61, 87
>skills/models, 74–76
Policy change: retention effect, 65
Political skills, 79–80
Political trends, 21–27
Politicization of higher education, 21–22
POWS (problems, objectives, workshops) model, 75
Practicums, 54
Preadmission
>for disabled, 34
>role in recruitment/retention, 83
Preventive law, 50–51
Private colleges
>private financial support, 52
>student retention, 7
>state involvement, 22
Private financial support, 51–53
Productivity improvement, 41
Professional associations, 97, 98, 110–111
Professional development, 95–98
Program evaluation: student affairs, 44, 75, 85
Program planning/review, 67
Project RETAIN, 50
"Promotion squeeze," 13
Public colleges
>accountability, 22
>private financial support, 52

Q
Quality: recommendations for, 26–27
Quality of student life, 63
Questionnaires
>Student Descriptive Questionnaire, 45
>Student Development Task Inventory, 45

R

Recorders for disabled, 34
Recordkeeping, 76–77
Recruitment (see Student recruitment)
Reeducation, 15–16, 34
Reentry students, 30, 35, 84
Registration, 5, 6
Rehabilitation Act of 1973, 33
Religious traditions, 31
Remedial training need, 33
Research and evaluation skills, 80–81, 108
Research projects, 67
Residence life program development, 46
Resource management, 23, 54
RETAIN Project, 50
Retention
      California efforts, 2, 7
      planning, 46, 48–50
      strategies, 64–66
      student affairs role, 69, 83–84
Retraining, 15–16, 34
Retrenchment: student affairs role, 78–80
Role expectations, 16, 82
Role models, 29–30
Role perception: student affairs, 59–60

S

SAT score decline, 33
Scheduling flexibility, 30, 32, 35
Scholarship funds, 53
Schroeder planning model, 76
Scripps College: student retention, 2
Section 504, Rehabilitation Act, 33
Sex roles, 16–17, 40
Sexual harassment, 30
Skill development (see also Study skills)
      budgeting, 77–78
      human resource management, 78
      management, 73–78
      need for, 109–110
      organizational, 81–82, 89
      political, 79–80
      research and evaluation, 80–81
Social changes, 1, 11–19
Social science majors, 37

Socialization
    foreign students, 32
    relationship to retention, 49–50
    women, 17, 30
Sponsored research, 23
Staff development, 65, 95
State action/accountability, 22–23
State coordinating/governing board, 22
Stetson University
    POWS model, 75
    student affairs planning, 44
Strategic planning, 43
Stress
    cultural, 32
    family/job, 32
    social change, 18, 19, 40
Student activities: repackaging, 86
Student affairs
    accountability model, 55
    changing role, 83, 87–88, 98
    consumer orientation, 67–70
    external focus, 70–71
    funding problems, 55, 60
    goals, 82, 108
    history, 1, 57
    implications of social change, 15–19, 27
    institutional influence, 61–62
    legal issues, 24–25, 50–51
    management strategies, 54
    need for codification of rules, 51
    opposing motivations, 59–60
    philosophical basis, 5–6, 59, 68
    planning models, 75–76
    recommendations for student involvement, 26–27
    relationship to development/fund-raising, 52–53
    relationship to faculty, 58, 66–67, 71, 91
    relationship to institution, 2, 40, 48, 56–58, 62–66, 81–82,
       97, 107–110
    relationship to retention, 49–50
    research areas, 80–81
    response to consumerism, 39, 51
    response to nontraditional students, 35–36, 39–40, 84–85
    response to vocationalism, 37
    services, 5–7
Student affairs personnel
    advocate/advisor role, 8

    contemporary role, 7–9
    credentials, 92
    credibility, 67, 71, 82, 91, 101, 103, 108
    custodian role, 4–5
    disciplinarian role, 3–4
    educator role, 5–7
    entry-level competencies, 93–94
    evaluation skills, 80–81
    financial management skills, 77–78
    institutional integrator role, 3, 8–9, 27, 47, 57–72, 103
    management skills, 73–78, 97
    organizational skills, 81–82
    political skills, 79–80
    relationship to president, 79
    research and evaluation skills, 80–81
    skill development, 73–83, 96–97
    training, 89–93, 98
Student Affairs Program Evaluation Process, 75
Student-college relationship, 50
Student data collection, 44, 77
Student Descriptive Questionnaire, 45
Student development
    commitment to/model, 6–7
    definition, 100
    function, 99
    integration with administrative practice, 102–103
    involvement theory, 104–105
    sex role changes, 17
    success factor, 66
    theories, 68–69, 82, 99–101
Student Development Task Inventory, 45
Student financial aid
    accountability, 23
    flexibility, 13, 30, 32, 35
    provided by student affairs, 6
    role in retention, 65, 83
Student government, 86
Student involvement: developmental theory, 104–105
Student life emphasis, 50
Student media, 86
Student organizations, 25, 86
Student publications, 4
Student recruitment, 12, 47–48, 63–64, 66, 69, 83–84
Student research, 67
Student retention (see Retention)
Student rights, 24–25, 38

Student services (see Student affairs)
Students
    academically underprepared, 11, 33, 36, 85
    changes, 2, 29–40
    characteristics, 36–40
    commuter, 27, 46, 84
    demand for services, 68–69
    disabled, 11, 33–34, 36, 84
    diversity: developmental issues, 101–102
    expectations, 12, 14
    international, 31–32, 35
    involvement in the institution, 2–3, 26–27, 104
    minorities, 30–31, 35, 84
    narcissism, 17–18, 38
    needs assessment, 45, 64
    older, 30, 34–35
    part-time, 27, 32–33, 36, 84
    persister vs. nonpersister, 64
    personal success motivation, 37–38
    research on, 80–81
    traditional vs. nontraditional age, 11–12, 29
    vocationalism, 36–37
    women, 29–30, 35, 84
Study skills, 48, 63
Success motivation, 37–38
Summer jobs, 54
Sun belt, 14
Support groups, 30
Support services
    evening/weekend, 32
    nontraditional students, 84
    role in retention, 83
SWOTS program assessment model, 75

T
Time management, 78
Tomorrow's Higher Education Project, 6, 69
Training: student personnel professionals, 89–93, 110–111
Transfer prevention, 50
Transportation needs: disabled, 34
Tutors (colonial), 3

U
Underprepared students, 11, 33, 36, 48, 85
University of Georgia: underprepared students, 85
University of Iowa: underprepared students, 33

University of Maryland: adult students, 7, 35
University of Maine at Farmington: faculty/student affairs
    relationship, 67
University of Nebraska: student affairs evaluation, 75, 85

V
Values
    challenges to, 18
    changing, 37, 40
    development of, 86–87
    older students, 34
    relationship to student activities, 83
    student affairs vs. institutional, 108
Vocationalism, 36–37, 85

W
Weekend programs, 48
Western theory of human behavior, 31
Women
    as student population, 11, 29–30, 35, 37, 84
    human development theory, 101
    inclusion in curricula, 91
    nontraditional careers, 16
    summer management program, 97
Workforce changes, 15
Workshops: career planning, 85
Writing skills, 33

Y
"Youth culture," 13

ASHE-ERIC HIGHER EDUCATION REPORTS

Starting in 1983, the Association for the Study of Higher Education assumed cosponsorship of the Higher Education Reports with the ERIC Clearinghouse on Higher Education. For the previous 11 years, ERIC and the American Association for Higher Education prepared and published the reports.

Each report is the definitive analysis of a tough higher education problem, based on a thorough research of pertinent literature and institutional experiences. Report topics, identified by a national survey, are written by noted practitioners and scholars with prepublication manuscript reviews by experts.

Eight monographs (10 monographs before 1985) in the ASHE-ERIC Higher Education Report series are published each year, available individually or by subscription. Subscription to eight issues is $55 regular; $40 for members of AERA, AAHE and AIR: $35 for members of ASHE. (Add $7.50 outside the United States.)

Prices for single copies, including 4th class postage and handling, are $7.50 regular and $6.00 for members of AERA, AAHE, AIR, and ASHE ($6.50 regular and $5.00 for members for reports published before 1983). If faster 1st class postage is desired for U.S. and Canadian orders, add $.75 for each publication ordered: overseas, add $4.50. For VISA and MasterCard payments, include card number, expiration date, and signature. Orders under $25 must be prepaid. Bulk discounts are available on orders of 15 or more reports (not applicable to subscriptions). Order from the Publications Department, Association for the Study of Higher Education, One Dupont Circle, Suite 630, Washington, D.C. 20036, 202/296-2597. Write for a publication list of all the Higher Education Reports available.

1985 Higher Education Reports

1. Flexibility in Academic Staffing: Effective Policies and Practices
   Kenneth P. Mortimer, Marque Bagshaw, and Andrew T. Masland

2. Associations in Action: The Washington, D.C., Higher Education Community
   Harland G. Bloland

3. And on the Seventh Day: Faculty Consulting and Supplemental Income
   Carol M. Boyer and Darrell R. Lewis

4. Faculty Research Performance: Lessons from the Sciences and Social Sciences
   John W. Creswell

5. Academic Program Reviews: Institutional Approaches, Expectations, and Controversies
   Clifton F. Conrad and Richard F. Wilson

6. Students in Urban Settings: Achieving the Baccalaureate Degree
   Richard C. Richardson, Jr., and Louis W. Bender

7. Serving More Than Students: A Critical Need for College Student Personnel Services
   Peter H. Garland

1984 Higher Education Reports

1. Adult Learning: State Policies and Institutional Practices
   K. Patricia Cross and Anne-Marie McCartan

2. Student Stress: Effects and Solutions
   Neal A. Whitman, David C. Spendlove, and Claire H. Clark

3. Part-time Faculty: Higher Education at a Crossroads
   Judith M. Gappa

4. Sex Discrimination Law in Higher Education: The Lessons of the Past Decade
   J. Ralph Lindgren, Patti T. Ota, Perry A. Zirkel, and Nan Van Gieson

5. Faculty Freedoms and Institutional Accountability: Interactions and Conflicts
   Steven G. Olswang and Barbara A. Lee

6. The High-Technology Connection: Academic Industrial Cooperation for Economic Growth
   Lynn G. Johnson

7. Employee Educational Programs: Implications for Industry and Higher Education
   Suzanne W. Morse

8. Academic Libraries: The Changing Knowledge Centers of Colleges and Universities
   Barbara B. Moran

9. Futures Research and the Strategic Planning Process: Implications for Higher Education
   James L. Morrison, William L. Renfro, and Wayne I. Boucher

10. Faculty Workload: Research, Theory, and Interpretation
    Harold E. Yuker

1983 Higher Education Reports

1. The Path to Excellence: Quality Assurance in Higher Education
   Laurence R. Marcus, Anita O. Leone, and Edward D. Goldberg

2. Faculty Recruitment, Retention, and Fair Employment: Obligations and Opportunities
   John S. Waggaman

3. Meeting the Challenges: Developing Faculty Careers
   Michael C. T. Brookes and Katherine L. German

4. Raising Academic Standards: A Guide to Learning Improvement
   Ruth Talbott Keimig

5. Serving Learners at a Distance: A Guide to Program Practices
   Charles E. Feasley

6. Competence, Admissions, and Articulation: Returning to the Basics in Higher Education
   Jean L. Preer

7. Public Service in Higher Education: Practices and Priorities
   Patricia H. Crosson

8. Academic Employment and Retrenchment: Judicial Review and
   Administrative Action
   Robert M. Hendrickson and Barbara A. Lee

9. Burnout: The New Academic Disease
   Winifred Albizu Meléndez and Rafael M. de Guzmán

10. Academic Workplace: New Demands, Heightened Tensions
    Ann E. Austin and Zelda F. Gamson